2009 The FBI Story

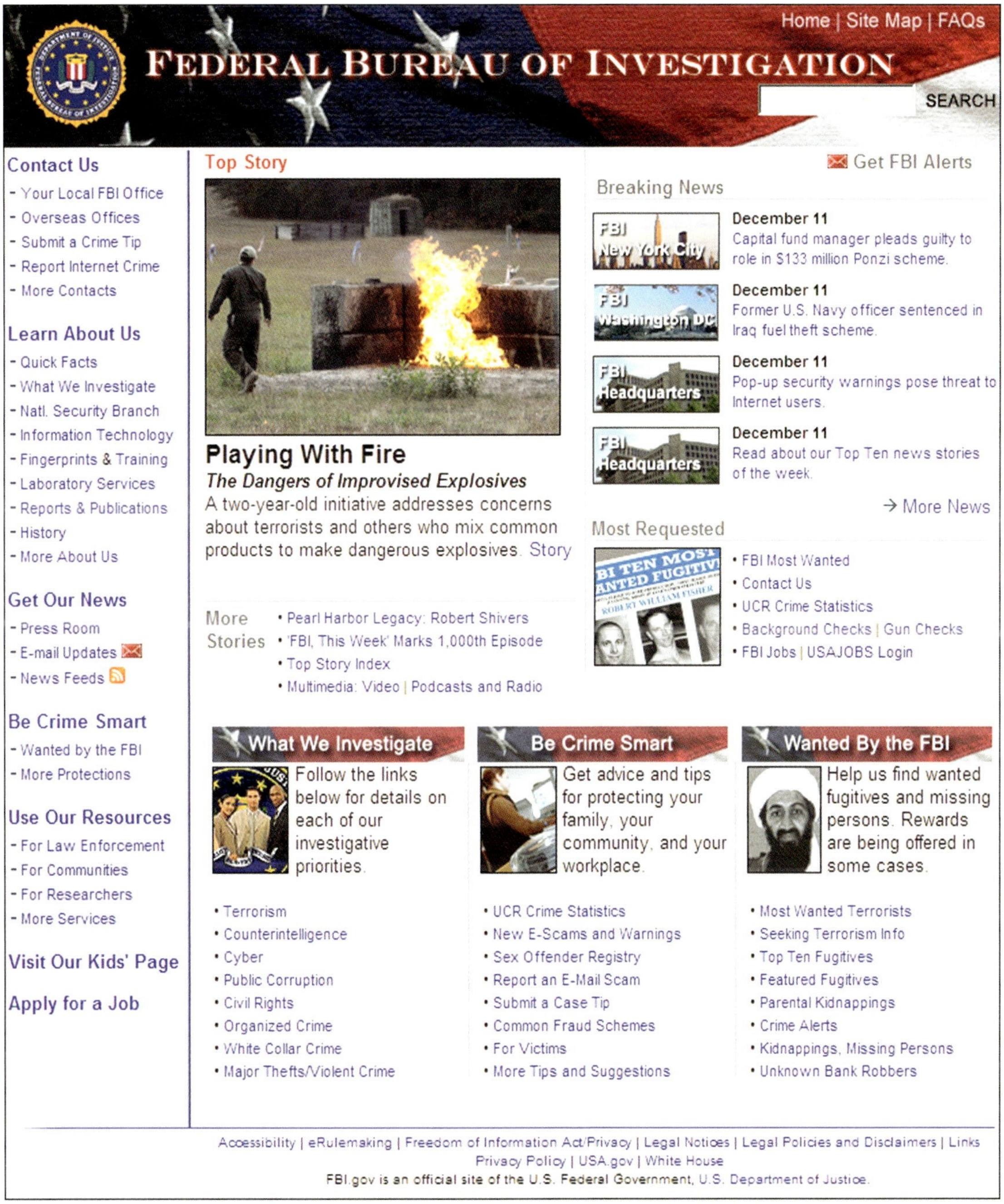
Home | Site Map | FAQs

FEDERAL BUREAU OF INVESTIGATION

SEARCH

Contact Us
- Your Local FBI Office
- Overseas Offices
- Submit a Crime Tip
- Report Internet Crime
- More Contacts

Learn About Us
- Quick Facts
- What We Investigate
- Natl. Security Branch
- Information Technology
- Fingerprints & Training
- Laboratory Services
- Reports & Publications
- History
- More About Us

Get Our News
- Press Room
- E-mail Updates
- News Feeds

Be Crime Smart
- Wanted by the FBI
- More Protections

Use Our Resources
- For Law Enforcement
- For Communities
- For Researchers
- More Services

Visit Our Kids' Page

Apply for a Job

Top Story

Playing With Fire
The Dangers of Improvised Explosives
A two-year-old initiative addresses concerns about terrorists and others who mix common products to make dangerous explosives. Story

More Stories
- Pearl Harbor Legacy: Robert Shivers
- 'FBI, This Week' Marks 1,000th Episode
- Top Story Index
- Multimedia: Video | Podcasts and Radio

Get FBI Alerts

Breaking News

FBI New York City — **December 11** Capital fund manager pleads guilty to role in $133 million Ponzi scheme.

FBI Washington DC — **December 11** Former U.S. Navy officer sentenced in Iraq fuel theft scheme.

FBI Headquarters — **December 11** Pop-up security warnings pose threat to Internet users.

FBI Headquarters — **December 11** Read about our Top Ten news stories of the week.

→ More News

Most Requested
- FBI Most Wanted
- Contact Us
- UCR Crime Statistics
- Background Checks | Gun Checks
- FBI Jobs | USAJOBS Login

What We Investigate
Follow the links below for details on each of our investigative priorities.
- Terrorism
- Counterintelligence
- Cyber
- Public Corruption
- Civil Rights
- Organized Crime
- White Collar Crime
- Major Thefts/Violent Crime

Be Crime Smart
Get advice and tips for protecting your family, your community, and your workplace.
- UCR Crime Statistics
- New E-Scams and Warnings
- Sex Offender Registry
- Report an E-Mail Scam
- Submit a Case Tip
- Common Fraud Schemes
- For Victims
- More Tips and Suggestions

Wanted By the FBI
Help us find wanted fugitives and missing persons. Rewards are being offered in some cases.
- Most Wanted Terrorists
- Seeking Terrorism Info
- Top Ten Fugitives
- Featured Fugitives
- Parental Kidnappings
- Crime Alerts
- Kidnappings, Missing Persons
- Unknown Bank Robbers

Accessibility | eRulemaking | Freedom of Information Act/Privacy | Legal Notices | Legal Policies and Disclaimers | Links
Privacy Policy | USA.gov | White House
FBI.gov is an official site of the U.S. Federal Government, U.S. Department of Justice.

A Message from FBI Director Robert S. Mueller, III

The year began with a major event requiring unprecedented security by an array of agencies—the inauguration of a new U.S. president. It came to an end with an attempted Christmas Day bombing of an airplane bound for Detroit. In between was a hate-filled attack on the Holocaust Museum, a tragic shooting at the Ft. Hood army base in Texas, and many other significant security issues and threats.

For the FBI and its partners, 2009 was one of the most challenging years in recent memory. A snapshot of what we faced and accomplished together—from stopping dangerous criminals to disrupting a wave of terror plots targeting everything from skyscrapers to synagogues—is captured in this latest edition of *The FBI Story*, a collection of news and feature articles from the Bureau's website. The book details emerging frauds and scams, major cyber takedowns and corruption busts, new initiatives involving highway serial killings and civil rights-era cold cases, and our latest Most Wanted fugitives and terrorists. It goes inside cutting edge forensic techniques and investigative technologies, joint international ventures targeting global gangs and online predators, and a handful of terrorism and spy cases. It even looks back at historic investigations that helped shape the FBI of today, including the hunt for gangsters like John Dillinger and Bonnie and Clyde during the pivotal year of 1934.

What is clear throughout these pages is that the threats to our homeland are as serious as ever. During the year, the FBI continued to build on its longstanding and post-9/11 investigative and intelligence capabilities, but more work remains to be done. In the months ahead, we must and will continue to adapt to ever-evolving threats, roll out new tools and technologies, and improve our programs, processes, and partnerships.

Thank you for your support, and we look forward to working with you and for you during 2010.

Director Mueller introduces President Barack Obama during his visit to FBI Headquarters on April 28, 2009.

WANTED BY THE FBI

Talented Professionals to Serve the Nation

Attention job seekers: the FBI is looking for a few good men and women to fill a variety of mission-critical roles within our organization.

Actually, we're looking for a few *thousand*—just over 2,100 professional staff employees and 850 special agents, to be precise—in one of the largest hiring blitzes in our 100-year history.

The reason behind our mega hiring initiative? According to Assistant Director John Raucci of our Human Resources Division, it's to bring more people on board with skills in critical areas, especially language fluency and computer science. "But," explains Raucci, "we're also looking for professionals in a wide variety of fields who have a deep desire to help protect our nation from terrorists, spies, and others who wish us harm."

All 2,100-plus jobs are now posted on our redesigned FBI Jobs website. The positions are located throughout the nation—in virtually every FBI field office and at our Headquarters in Washington, D.C. You must be a U.S. citizen to apply.

Who we are looking for. According to Raucci, besides those skilled in computers and foreign languages we also need experts in:

- Finance and accounting;
- Security;
- Intelligence analysis;
- Compliance and quality assurance;
- Training and education;
- Records management;
- Fingerprint examination;
- Information technology;
- Nursing and counseling;
- Physical surveillance;
- Electrical engineering;
- Physical/natural/social sciences;
- Administrative/clerical processes;
- Automotive mechanics; and
- Management/program analysis.

The process. On the FBI Jobs website, take a look at available positions. If you see a job you think you're qualified for, read our "How to Apply" page and then fill out the online application.

Applications will be vetted, and best qualified candidates will be contacted for interviews. We will arrange regional "mega career invitationals" to speed up that process—all selected candidates will gather at designated locations to be interviewed. Those who are ultimately offered a conditional job will be scheduled for their polygraphs, drug screenings, and employment briefings. Candidates who make it past that stage are then ready for the final step—their background investigations.

Our pre-employment background investigations are, by necessity, very thorough and take time, but we hope to have everyone hired and onboard by September 30, 2009. A hiring initiative of this magnitude requires a massive in-house response to quickly process the deluge of applications we expect to receive, so we're reallocating personnel who will be dedicated to this initiative.

If you aren't offered the specific job you have applied for but still meet the hiring criteria, your application will be kept on hand for possible consideration at a later time.

Interested in becoming a special agent? We also continue to recruit and process agent candidates. Since October 1, we have hired nearly 180 agents and plan to hire a total of 850 by the end of the fiscal year.

Like our professional staff applicants, we're looking for agent candidates with foreign language fluency (especially in Middle Eastern and Asian dialects) and computer science backgrounds, and those with skills in certified public accounting, tactics training, intelligence, law enforcement/military, engineering, law, and science.

Editor's note: the hiring blitz ended later in January.

January 12, 2009

Declining Crime Rates

According to the FBI's latest Preliminary Semiannual Uniform Crime Report, violent crime in the nation dropped 3.5 percent and property crime declined 2.5 percent during the first six months of 2008, compared to the same period in 2007.

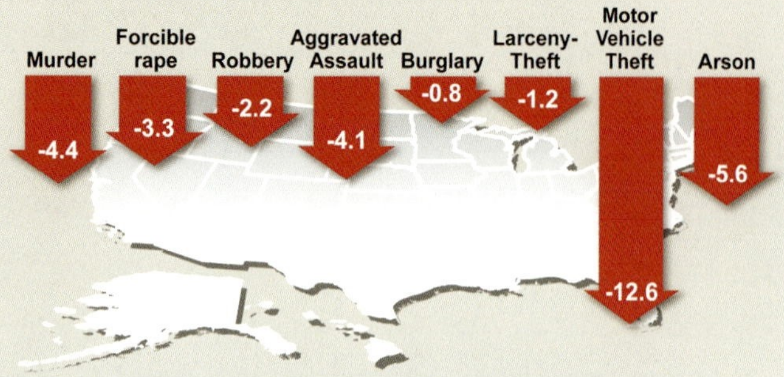

SOME GOOD NEWS

Crime is Declining

For the second year in a row, our *Preliminary Semiannual Uniform Crime Report* shows that violent crimes, property crimes, and arsons are declining.

Nationwide, violent crime fell 3.5 percent and property crime 2.5 percent during the first six months of the year; the full 2008 report will be available in the fall.

Each of the specific crimes measured by the Uniform Crime Reporting (UCR) Program—murder and non-negligent manslaughter, forcible rape, robbery, aggravated assault, burglary, larceny-theft, motor vehicle theft, and arson—decreased during the first half of 2008 as compared to the same time frame in 2007.

Here are some of the report's highlights:

- Violent crimes in all population groups declined: murder by 4.4 percent, aggravated assault by 4.1 percent, forcible rape by 3.3 percent, and robbery by 2.2 percent.
- On a regional basis, law enforcement in all four parts of the country reported a drop in violent crimes: 6.0 percent in the Midwest, 5.0 percent in the West, 2.9 percent in the Northeast, and 1.5 percent in the South.
- Overall, property crimes fell in the Midwest (4.7 percent), the West (6.1 percent), and the South (0.4 percent).
- Among population groupings, each category of property crime was down: motor vehicle thefts by 12.6 percent, larceny-theft by 1.2 percent, and burglaries by 0.8 percent.
- Arsons dropped in all four regions of the country and among all population groups (with the exception of cities with populations of 250,000-499,999, where it actually increased 2.0 percent).

But there were some specific increases noted:

- Murder and non-negligent manslaughter were up in mid-sized cities with populations of 50,000-99,999 (3.3 percent), along with smaller cities of populations under 10,000 (9.8 percent).
- In the Northeast, forcible rapes were up slightly (0.6 percent), as were burglaries (2.7 percent) and larceny-theft (2.9 percent) over the same six-month period in 2007.
- Cities with populations of one million-plus also recorded a 3.4 percent jump in forcible rapes.
- Property crimes rose in the Northeast by 1.7 percent.
- The South saw an increase in burglaries (0.6 percent) and larceny-thefts (0.5 percent).

Did you ever wonder why the UCR program collects offense statistics on only those eight particular crimes? It's because they are serious crimes that occur most frequently and come to the attention of state and local law enforcement most often.

Special thanks to our state and local law enforcement partners from the 11,515 agencies that contributed to this report. And as we caution each year, please don't draw conclusions of our data by making direct comparisons between cities—valid assessments are possible ONLY with careful study and analysis of the range of unique conditions affecting each local law enforcement jurisdiction.

Why do we compile the statistics, then? To help law enforcement, legislators, and communities better understand and fight crime.

COMBATING CYBER CRIME

Global Network Operates 24/7

Cyber crooks have become so organized and businesslike that they use online forums to advertise illegal wares, buy and sell computer viruses, and traffic in stolen identities—all for huge profits.

Besides fueling an underground criminal economy, the Internet is increasingly being exploited by terrorists and spies, the FBI's top cyber experts said at a recent international conference on cyber security.

For about $30, one of our undercover agents explained, cyber crooks anywhere in the world can buy a blank credit card, complete with the holographic security markings used by legitimate credit card companies. They can buy equipment to encode someone's stolen identity information onto the card. And they can buy software to verify that the unsuspecting victim's credit is good, so that anyone using the phony card will not raise suspicions at the checkout counter.

"The sophistication of our adversaries is growing," Shawn Henry, head of our Cyber Division, told about 400 participants from 37 countries at the first International Conference on Cyber Security. The conference was held last week at Fordham University in New York City and was sponsored by the university and our New York office, bringing together our cyber experts and their international counterparts from law enforcement, industry, government, and academia.

The three-day event, which featured a variety of speakers and panel discussions, was organized to find global solutions to emerging cyber threats. "The FBI's goal of sponsoring this conference is to build and forge long-lasting relationships to combat terrorist and criminal use of the Internet," said Joseph Demarest, who heads our New York office. "The conference is the beginning of greater cooperation on all cyber matters."

The key to fighting cyber crime, conference participants agreed, is through international cooperation.

A good example of that cooperation is today's international 24/7 network of cyber investigators. The network, established among the G8 nations in 1997, has since grown to 55 member countries, all of which have dedicated cyber crime investigators who can respond to fast-moving cases at a moment's notice—often with

An FBI cyber executive addresses the conference.

the ability to "fast freeze" e-mail traffic and other stored electronic data, which can preserve a crook's otherwise fleeting digital footprint.

Here's a hypothetical example of how the network operates: A cyber crook hacks into a bank in Mexico City. Mexican investigators trace the computer used in the attack to New York City and quickly contact FBI agents, who discover that the New York computer is linked to a computer in South Korea. They alert Korean agents, who learn that the attack originated in Bangkok. Thai agents make the arrest. Thanks to the network, the investigative process may take hours or days instead of weeks or months.

This level of timely cooperation is essential. But cooperation needs to go hand in hand with consistent laws for cyber crimes, said Christopher Painter, Deputy Assistant Director of our Cyber Division. Uniform penalties must be adopted, or savvy cyber crooks will simply base their operations in countries with the most lax cyber laws.

"The bottom line is to make sure there are consequences for criminal cyber actions and similar consequences everywhere," Painter explained. "The bad guys need to know there is no free ride."

Left: FBI Director Mueller gets the latest intelligence on national security from one of his daily briefers.

PROTECTING NATIONAL SECURITY

One Briefing at a Time

"It's pretty amazing to know that after I provided information to Director Mueller, he turned around and gave it to the President."

This—according to Jennifer, one of our intelligence briefers—is one good reason why she feels a sense of accomplishment at the end of a day on the job. It's heady stuff: playing a small but vital role in the national security decision-making process at the highest levels of our government.

We have several such briefers at any given time—experienced analysts who typically spend a year briefing the FBI Director, the U.S. Attorney General, and both of their executive staffs, covering the full range of our priorities but focusing on national security matters.

Among the briefers' duties: sifting through mountains of raw intelligence, investigative reports, analytical reports, open source material, and intelligence assessments—from both from the Bureau and our intelligence community partners—and then delivering clear and concise presentations on the most relevant information.

For more details on their roles, we went straight to the source—current and former FBI briefers. Here's some of what they had to say:

Best part of the job?

"Seeing up close the real contribution that the FBI makes to combat terrorism in the U.S. and around the globe—and playing a part in that," says John.

For Jennifer, it's knowing that "policy discussions are being deliberated based on the intelligence you've provided."

It's participating in the unfolding intelligence cycle—"how intelligence is created by the intel community and consumed by senior cabinet members," explains Jed.

Most challenging aspect?

"Working night shift hours—but overall, the amazing experience of briefing the executives is worth the sleep sacrifice!" says Ayn.

According to Lucian, "The series of morning briefings are fast-paced, intense, and stressful...the long hours of continual preparation are exhausting...but there is immense satisfaction in knowing one's words assist executives in making critical decisions."

What makes a good briefer?

"Excellent analytical abilities," says Pradeep, "along with strong oral and written skills, and definitely the ability to be decisive and calm under demanding time constraints."

Brian believes you have to be a straight-shooter: "If you don't know the answer to a question, you have to look the executive in the eye and say 'I don't know, but I will find out for you.' And then find out."

The bottom line. FBI briefers—who not only work with representatives from across Bureau programs but also with fellow briefers at other agencies—make sure vital intelligence gets to the people in a position to act upon it. Explains Jason, "We're brokers of information...we provide senior FBI officials and our partner intelligence agencies with the facts and perspectives they need to get the job done."

And FBI national security executive Phil Mudd adds, "It's hard to overestimate the importance of briefers...they not only present facts but help us understand context. They describe problems and outline opportunities in ways that give the Department of Justice and the FBI teams a concise way to start every day. We could not succeed without them, their talent, and their dedication."

If you like what you hear—and are interested in joining the FBI as an analyst and possibly as a future briefer—it's a good time to apply. We've just posted more than 2,100 professional staff jobs, including analyst positions, on our FBI Jobs website.

INAUGURAL SECURITY

Behind the Scenes

As Barack Obama took the oath of office to become the 44th President of the United States, the men and women in our Command and Tactical Operations Center paused briefly to witness the historic occasion on flat screens around the room—but only briefly. Then it was back to the business of communicating with agents in the field and our partners at other command posts around the city to continue to monitor the event and to assess any possible threats.

Millions of people arrived in Washington almost overnight for inaugural activities, but we started planning security with our law enforcement partners six months ago. Our 24/7 security coverage began January 17 and continued throughout the festivities.

The Secret Service is on point for protecting the President and takes the lead for inaugural security, but issues involving terrorism, weapons of mass destruction, and crisis management are the FBI's responsibility.

From the command center at our Washington Field Office, agents, analysts, administrators, and members of our Joint Terrorism Task Force fielded tips from the public and used sophisticated mapping and surveillance technology to track suspicious activity as well as to monitor our response teams on the ground near the Capitol and the inaugural parade route along Pennsylvania Avenue.

More than 150 plainclothes teams on foot and in vehicles were "our eyes and ears on the ground—our trip wires, if you will," said John Perren, Special Agent in Charge of our Counterterrorism Division at our Washington office. The teams were looking for anything suspicious—an abandoned backpack at a Metro station that could be a bomb, an unknown liquid in a plastic bottle that might be a weapon of mass destruction. If necessary, ground teams could also quickly respond to a crisis situation.

The command center—the hub of FBI communications activity—enabled teams in the field to share information in real time and allowed its staff to continually update the threat assessment. Manning the operation were some of the Bureau's most "battle-tested" personnel, said Joseph Persichini, Jr., who heads the Washington Field Office. "Many people in the room were here during 9/11 and responded to the Pentagon after the attacks," he said. "Our team is phenomenal."

The Washington Field Office's tactical command center coordinated the FBI's role during the presidential inauguration.

But every major event is different, he added, and despite the fact that our extensive intelligence gathering revealed no credible threats prior to Inauguration Day, the command post responded immediately to multiple threats. Our intelligence assets from around the world were put into play to "run any threats to the ground," Perren said.

Meanwhile, over at the Joint Information Center run by the U.S. Secret Service, more than 20 agencies handled all the media for security issues. "We got every call under the sun," said Richard Kolko, who along with Jason Pack represented the FBI at the center.

Later in the day, as President Obama made his way down Pennsylvania Avenue on his way to the White House, flanked by what may be a record number of onlookers, one of our agents on the street praised the cooperation between our law enforcement partners and all the behind-the-scenes efforts that went into not only the President's security but the public's safety.

"It's a good feeling," he said, "that our work allowed people to celebrate this historic event without any major security incidents."

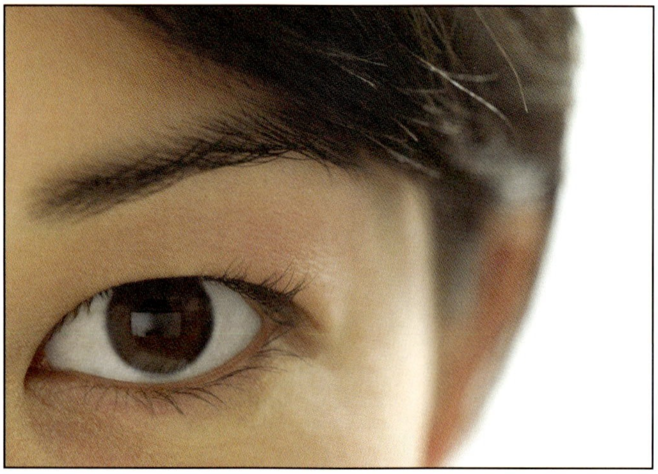

BEYOND FINGERPRINTS

Our New Identification System

Palm prints are taken from the scene of a diffused roadside bomb in Iraq. Later, an individual entering a New York airport is arrested on an unrelated charge. A full set of prints are taken during the booking process and submitted to our Next Generation Identification (NGI) system. A positive ID connects the man to the roadside bomb.

A ski mask-wearing bank robber leaves with his loot, and witnesses tell police they noticed a red skull tattoo on his hand. A search of NGI's Interstate Photo System for a red skull tattoo provides a potential candidate list that could ultimately lead to the identification of the bank robber.

Both cases are hypothetical, but in the not-too-distant future these scenarios could really happen…thanks to the ongoing development of the Next Generation Identification system—a logical evolution of our current Integrated Automated Fingerprint Identification System (IAFIS).

That evolution will include not only enhanced fingerprint capabilities but also other forms of biometric identification like palm prints, iris scans, facial imaging, scars, marks, and tattoos—in one searchable system.

Next Generation Identification is…

A state-of-the-art identification system that will be "bigger, faster, and better" than IAFIS, says Assistant Director Tom Bush of our Criminal Justice Information Services Division.

"Bigger" because it will increase the capacity of our fingerprint storage plus house multimodal biometrics records like palm prints and iris scans…and still have room to accommodate future biometric technologies (i.e., voice, gait, etc.) as they become available and prove reliable.

"Faster" because it will speed up response time for high priority criminal ten-print submissions from two hours to about 10 minutes on average. There will also be a special category called the "Repository of Individuals of Special Concern" containing records of known or suspected terrorists, wanted persons, and sexual offender registry names. These records can be quickly searched to help law enforcement in the U.S. and American soldiers in places like Iraq and Afghanistan assess the level of threat during an encounter.

"Better" because going beyond fingerprints as biometric identifiers will enhance the investigative and identification processes. For example, adding palm prints makes sense: some of the latent prints left behind by criminals at crime scenes are palm prints. NGI is also being developed to be compatible with other U.S. biometric systems and potentially with those of some foreign partners.

Next Generation Identification is not…

A tool to expand the categories of individuals from who the fingerprints and biometric data may be collected, nor will it change existing legal authorities.

It doesn't threaten individual privacy. As required with any federal system, the FBI is doing Privacy Impact Assessments on what information will be collected, how it will be shared, how it will be accessed, and how the data will be securely stored…all in an effort to protect privacy.

NGI is not strictly an FBI system. It's a joint effort and is being developed in full collaboration with its primary users—our local, state, and federal partners…in particular the CJIS Advisory Policy Board and the National Crime Prevention Compact Council.

Over the next few years, we'll be rolling out NGI capabilities incrementally so our partners will have the benefit of each capability as soon as it gets our stamp of approval.

FBI MEDICS

Special Agents with Special Skills

Our investigators and critical response professionals often find themselves in harm's way—working in a war zone, serving warrants on dangerous criminals, hunting down terrorists, responding to the potential use of a chemical or biological agent.

For our employees, the possibility of injury or illness is real—and many times medical facilities are nowhere nearby or don't provide the kind of security or care we need.

That's why we've created our own cadre of highly trained FBI medics.

A bit of history. Our Emergency Medical Support Program, headed by Dr. William Fabbri, was launched in the wake of the 1998 U.S. Embassy bombings in East Africa. Explains Dr. Fabbri, "After that investigation, we realized that our teams of people working in austere medical environments were at risk. And because operational deployments include a limited number of personnel—situations where even one minor injury or temporary illness could impact our mission—we began including FBI medics on our deployment teams."

Today, our medics support crisis response efforts, special operations, and terrorism and high-risk investigations here and abroad. Their patients are not just FBI employees—for example, our medics will tend to subjects and civilians involved in a hostage situation where it's not safe for local emergency workers to enter the scene.

And when needed, our medics are supported by Bureau doctors, physician assistants, nurses, and contractors.

We have over 250 special agent medics around the country who are fully qualified emergency medical specialists—EMTs, advanced paramedics, emergency physicians, etc. Most come to us with years of emergency medicine experience, and they continue to train to keep their skills sharp. They are embedded within certain field SWAT teams, our Hazardous Materials Response Unit in the FBI Laboratory, and our Hostage Rescue Team in our Critical Incident Response Group.

Why are our medics agents? So that in between answering sick calls and checking the safety of local water supplies, they can also conduct interviews and recover evidence.

Being an FBI medic can be challenging. Dr. Fabbri recalls when water testing by a Bureau paramedic detected sewage contamination, preventing illness during an overseas investigation. He also remembers the work of our medics during the 2002 Salt Lake City Winter Olympics deployment of 1,600 FBI personnel, in close quarters with some 1.5 million visitors, at the height of flu season!

A team of FBI medics transport a Bureau employee in need of medical attention during an operational deployment.

But it's also a memorable job:

- A medic from Los Angeles, a physician trained in emergency medicine, recalls "serving as an intermediary between U.S. authorities and Chinese doctors after the stabbing of an American couple at last summer's Beijing Olympics."
- One of our New York medics tells of a deployment to a West African nation wracked by civil war that left the country's infrastructure in shambles—no power, sewer, or running water outside of the U.S. Embassy. "I assisted our Evidence Response Team while promoting the health and safety of the rest of the team by mitigating animal, food and water, mechanical, and physical hazards," he says.
- Another medic from Columbia remembers "taking care of three FBI personnel working at the G-8 Summit who developed kidney stones almost at the same time!"
- And a medic in our Washington Field Office says his most memorable contribution occurred after 9/11—"the scenes at Ground Zero and the New York City morgue and doing my best to support our personnel in the midst of a chaotic situation."

Says Dr. Fabbri, "FBI medics protect our people so they can continue protecting the American public."

January 30, 2009

DIGITAL BILLBOARDS

What a Difference a Year Makes

For years we've prominently posted wanted fugitives and missing persons here on our website for all the world to see…and enlisted the help of the news media in spreading the word about them far and wide.

Still, when we were approached in 2007 by an exec from Clear Channel Outdoor who offered to provide space on their collection of digital billboards nationwide to help catch crooks and rescue kidnapped kids—as a public service—we jumped at the chance.

And why not. The exposure on the highways and byways of America's big cities delivers lots of eyeballs. And as our Public Affairs Assistant Director John Miller says, "These are not your father's billboards." That's right: they are digitized. And like a computer screen, they can be changed at a moment's notice—quite handy when time is of the essence and you're searching for that missing teen or dangerous felon.

And so, just over a year ago, we joined with Clear Channel in launching the digital billboard initiative in 20 cities across the country. Since then, we've added three more partners: Adams Outdoor, Lamar Advertising, and the Outdoor Advertising Association of Georgia. That gives us access to more than 1,000 digital billboards nationwide today.

So what has a year wrought? Most importantly, the billboards have led directly to the capture of at least 14 fugitives, plus many more indirectly through our overall publicity efforts. And all at essentially no cost to the American taxpayer.

Left: A digital billboard on the U.S.-Mexico border

Here are just a few of the ways we've successfully tapped into the digital billboards with our partners:

- On November 12, 2008, Richard Franklin Wiggins, Jr. was arrested for money laundering and for ties to a drug trafficking organization—just three weeks after both Lamar Advertising and Adams Outdoor ran his image on their digital billboards in the Norfolk, Virginia area. Wiggins reportedly turned himself in at the insistence of his family and friends.
- On October 24, 2008, Walter Haskell was arrested for an armed robbery in New Jersey that he had committed several months earlier. After the robbery, he fled to Minnesota. His image was plastered on digital billboards across the state, generating tips that led to his apprehension. "If we have a crack at over a quarter-million people seeing that photo every day, then we have a very good chance at catching the person we're after," said Special Agent Sean Quinn, a spokesman for the FBI in Newark. "The exposure gets us started."
- Our digital billboard partners activated their networks on short notice when we announced two additions last year to our Ten Most Wanted Fugitives list: Michael Jason Registe on July 28 and Edward Eugene Harper on November 29.
- On November 9, 2008, Christopher Ellis was apprehended for a multi-state crime spree that included a bank robbery in Kentucky, a kidnapping and carjacking in Georgia, and a home invasion in Tennessee. Our partners placed a photo of Ellis and the truck he was driving on billboards in multiple states across the region. The publicity generated by the digital billboards contributed to a larger campaign which generated the tip that led to his arrest.

Long story short: the billboards are working and working well. And that means a safer America for all.

ALL IN THE FAMILY
Spy and His Son Indicted

In a spy case eerily reminiscent of one from more than two decades ago, a federal indictment was unsealed January 29 charging a father and son with conspiracy against the United States.

Harold J. Nicholson—a former CIA employee—and his 24-year-old son Nathaniel were charged in Portland, Oregon with two counts of conspiracy, one count of acting as an agent of a foreign government (in this case, Russia), and four counts of money laundering.

As you might remember, another father and son team—John and Michael Walker—were charged in 1985 with spying for the Soviet Union. (Walker also brought his brother Arthur into the fold.)

The kicker in all this? Harold Nicholson is already in prison, serving a more than 23-year sentence at the Federal Correctional Institution in Sheridan, Oregon for his 1997 conviction on charges of conspiring to commit espionage for the Russian Federation.

Being behind bars, though, apparently didn't stop Nicholson—he allegedly continued his attempts at maintaining his relationship with the Russians through his son.

How he did it. According to charges, Harold Nicholson felt he was owed additional payment from his Russian handlers for the classified national defense information he provided them during the 1990s. He may have first attempted to communicate with his handlers through fellow prisoners in the year 2000 by convincing the inmates to have visiting family members or friends mail letters for him. Later on, he was more successful in convincing a soon-to-be-released inmate to mail a package for him.

In addition to wanting his Russian "pension"—as he termed it—for services rendered, Nicholson believed he still had sensitive information that would be of use to his handlers but was afraid the information would soon become stale and worthless.

Partners in crime. According to a court affidavit, by 2006 Nicholson had turned his focus to his son Nathaniel, communicating with him through the limited means available in prison—letters, telephone calls, and visits—to garner his assistance as a go-between. It worked: beginning in December 2006, Nathaniel took the first of many overseas trips on behalf of his father—

Harold James Nicholson

the first to Mexico City, where we believe he met with Russian intelligence officials, passed information from his father, and received money.

Over time, Nicholson allegedly instructed his son on how to collect money from the Russians in a covert and secretive manner, how to avoid detection by law enforcement, and how to avoid international currency reporting requirements upon returning to the States with U.S. currency from Russian handlers.

Court documents show that Nathaniel took a series of trips from December 2006 to December 2008 to meet with agents of the Russian Federation in San Francisco; Mexico City, Mexico; Lima, Peru; and Cyprus. He allegedly collected money while on these trips and received additional instructions from his handlers. He then brought the money back to Oregon to disperse to family members…at the direction of his father.

The indictment against the two men also seeks forfeiture of the money given to Nathaniel Nicholson by the Russian Federation, alleged to be the proceeds of his father's past espionage activities.

Left: Patty Hearst robbing a San Francisco bank on April 15, 1974.

A BYTE OUT OF HISTORY

The Patty Hearst Kidnapping

Around 9 o'clock in the evening on February 4, 1974—35 years ago today—there was a knock on the door of apartment #4 at 2603 Benvenue Street in Berkeley, California. In burst a group of men and women with their guns drawn. They grabbed a surprised 19-year-old college student named Patty Hearst, beat up her fiancé, threw her in the trunk of their car, and drove off.

Thus began one of the strangest cases in FBI history. Hearst, it was soon discovered, had been kidnapped by a group of armed radicals that billed themselves as the Symbionese Liberation Army, or SLA. Led by a hardened criminal named Donald DeFreeze, the SLA wanted nothing less than to incite a guerrilla war against the U.S. government and destroy what they called the "capitalist state." Their ranks included women and men, blacks and whites, and anarchists and extremists from various walks in life.

Why'd they snatch Hearst? To get the country's attention, primarily. Hearst was from a wealthy, powerful family—her grandfather was the newspaper magnate William Randolph Hearst. The SLA's plan worked and worked well: the kidnapping stunned the country and made front-page national news.

But the SLA had more plans for Patty Hearst. Soon after her disappearance, the SLA began releasing audiotapes demanding millions of dollars in food donations in exchange for her release. At the same time, they apparently began abusing and brainwashing their captive, hoping to turn this young heiress from the highest reaches of society into a poster child for their coming revolution.

That, too, seemed to work. On April 3, 1974, the SLA released a tape with Hearst saying that she'd joined their fight to free the oppressed and had even taken a new name. A dozen days later, she was spotted on bank surveillance cameras wielding an assault weapon during an SLA bank robbery, barking orders to bystanders and providing cover to her confederates.

Meanwhile, the FBI had launched one of the most massive, agent-intensive searches in its history to find Hearst and stop the SLA. Working with many partners, the Bureau ran down thousands of leads. But with the SLA frightening potential informants into silence, using good operational security, and relying on an organized network of safe houses, it was tough going.

A break came in Los Angeles. On May 16, two SLA members tried to steal an ammunition belt from a local store and were nearly caught. The getaway van was discovered, which led authorities to an SLA safe house. The next day, it was surrounded by L.A. police. A massive shootout ensued and the building went up in flames. Six members of the SLA died in the blaze, including DeFreeze.

But where was Hearst? She and several others had escaped and began traveling around the country to avoid capture. FBI agents, though, were close behind. Hearst was finally captured in San Francisco on September 18, 1975 and charged with bank robbery and other crimes.

Her trial was as sensational as the chase. Despite claims of brainwashing, the jury found her guilty, and she was sentenced to seven years in prison. She served two years before President Carter commuted her sentence. She was later pardoned.

And the rest of the SLA? The FBI caught up with them all. The last two members were arrested in 1999 and 2002. Case closed.

THE GANG THREAT

Get Educated

Gangs are morphing, multiplying, and migrating—entrenching themselves not just in our inner cites but increasingly in our ever-sprawling suburbs and wide-open rural spaces.

In some communities, they are responsible for as much as a staggering 80 percent of all crimes. They are selling drugs to your kids, shooting up your neighborhoods, invading your homes, robbing your banks and stores, stealing your identities and money, and sowing plenty of fear and violence along the way.

There are gangs in the military...gangs in prison...gangs all over the Internet (recruiting, communicating, intimidating)...gangs on Native American reservations...and gangs on motorcycles roving the countryside. More and more women are joining gangs, too, sometimes leading their own subsets of larger criminal groups.

At last count (this past September), our nation had **at least 20,000 gangs** with **at least one million total members** from coast to coast.

These conclusions—and many more—are all part of the just released National Gang Threat Assessment 2009.

Now matter how you slice it—locally, regionally, nationally—it's a sobering portrait. And well worth reading for its insights, statistics, and predictions...whether you are a law enforcement professional, a community leader, an educator, a social services provider, or just a concerned citizen.

The report is based on law enforcement's collective intelligence—the product specifically of the National Gang Intelligence Center, the National Drug Intelligence Center, and a host of other local, state, and federal agencies.

Besides contributing to this report, we in the FBI—working with our partners more closely than ever—continue to put a lot of time, energy, and resources into tackling the growing gang threat. That includes:

- Synthesizing information on gangs from around the nation and even from around the globe (largely through the National Gang Intelligence Center) and pushing that out as intelligence assessments to our law enforcement partners to help them make cases and get a better handle on local threats;

- Leading the multi-agency MS-13 National Gang Task Force, which coordinates investigations and prosecutions of this extremely violent gang, including with law enforcement officials in Central America, its birthplace overseas;
- Taking part in the Department of Justice's National Gang Targeting Enforcement and Coordination Center, or GangTECC, a task force that looks for ways to make the most impact through multi-jurisdictional investigations involving federal law enforcement; and
- Putting boots on the ground, so speak—hundreds of highly trained special agents nationwide who work to dismantle gangs from the top down through more than 200 multi-agency Safe Streets Task Forces, including about 150 that specifically target gangs.

Of course, we need your help. Please report crimes and potential criminal activity to us. Please be alert to common gang warning signs in your children and in your neighborhoods. And please get involved and stay involved in anti-gang activities and proactive outreach initiatives in your community.

International Crackdown on Child Pornography Rings

What started in 2006 with one case in Australia spread throughout Europe and to the United States. In all, Operation Koala and Joint Hammer involved 28 countries and resulted in the dismantling of seven major global online child pornography rings.

In the United States, investigators have followed leads nationwide. As a result, young victims of sexual exploitation have been rescued, and more than 60 people have been arrested on a variety of pornography and sexual exploitation charges. The investigation is ongoing.

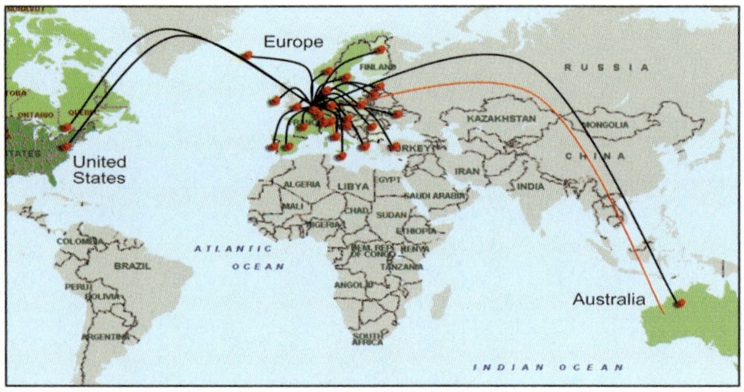

RESCUING OUR CHILDREN

Seven Massive Porn Rings Dismantled

What started as a tip from Australian authorities in 2006 regarding a sexually explicit video has turned into one of the largest global child pornography investigations on record—and a model for how law enforcement cooperation can cast a powerful light into the darkest reaches of the Internet to bring child predators to justice.

Operation Joint Hammer has resulted in the rescue of 14 girls—some as young as 3 years old—who were being sexually abused by pornographers. Approximately 170 people have been arrested, more than 60 of them U.S. citizens. Seven major child pornography rings, hosting the worst of the worst, have been dismantled. And the investigation is far from complete.

Working with international law enforcement organizations, members of our Innocent Images National Initiative program are playing a key role in the operation, along with the Department of Justice (DOJ), the United States Postal Inspection Service (USPIS), and U.S. Immigration and Customs Enforcement (ICE).

Here is what happened: Authorities in Queensland, Australia came across a pornographic video online showing a young victim. This victim was determined to be Dutch with a Flemish accent. Authorities in Belgium were contacted, and the ensuing European investigation became known as Operation Koala.

Belgian police identified and arrested the molester, who provided information about the video's producer, an Italian national who ran a pornographic website. When Italian police arrested the producer and shut down his website, they retrieved 50,000 e-mails to the porn site. Those e-mails formed the basis of Operation Joint Hammer. They were routed by Europol to the 28 countries from which they originated—with more than 11,000 coming from the United States.

The Innocent Images Operations Unit, along with our U.S. partners, quickly got to work. From the U.S. e-mails, about 700 became workable investigative leads. These were divided between the FBI, USPIS, and ICE. DOJ's Child Exploitation and Obscenity Section, responsible for prosecuting the federal cases, also played a critical role. As the investigation proceeded, many of our state and local law enforcement partners participated, conducting searches and making arrests.

The investigation is ongoing, but already dangerous sexual predators have been stopped:

- A New Jersey man pled guilty to producing sexual images of his 9-year-old daughter. Evidence seized during the search of his home revealed that he had nearly 130,000 images of child pornography. He was sentenced to almost 20 years in prison.
- An Arizona fifth-grade schoolteacher was a customer of the Italian pornography website. A search of his home resulted in allegations of sexual contact with female students at his school. He faces multiple charges of sexual exploitation of children.
- A convicted sex offender from Philadelphia who spent 15 years in prison for molesting children was charged with advertising, distributing, and receiving child pornography. Evidence indicates that he administered two major global online child pornography bulletin boards.

So far, the FBI and our U.S. partners have conducted more than 250 searches as part of the operation. "We're still working our way through all the cases," said our agent in charge of the investigation.

"Cooperation is the key," the agent added. "During our regular meetings with postal inspectors, ICE, and DOJ, we do whatever needs to be done as a team to make sure the cases keep moving forward."

MOBSTER ON THE RUN

'Whitey' Bulger Search Continues Overseas

Supervisory Special Agent Richard Teahan, who heads the Bulger Fugitive Task Force in Boston, speaks at the Foreign Press Center.

One of the FBI's most notorious fugitives was in the spotlight yesterday, as a briefing for international media at the State Department offered a global perspective on James "Whitey" Bulger, the Boston crime boss wanted for his role in 19 murders and a host of other offenses.

Because Bulger is believed to be living overseas, "the focus of the case has become international," said Richard Teahan, a Supervisory Special Agent in our Boston office who is in charge of the case. Through international exposure, Teahan said, "We hope to make his world smaller for him."

There is currently a reward of up to $2 million for Bulger, the largest reward we've ever offered for any of our U.S. Top Ten fugitives.

The job of catching Bulger—on the run for 14 years—has not been easy, in part because he is a meticulous planner who spent nearly two decades preparing for life as a fugitive. He stashed money all over the world, and he leaves no paper trail, paying only in cash.

Based on intelligence, we have a strong picture of Bulger's personality:

- He is an avid reader who frequents libraries, an animal lover, and a fitness nut who takes long walks.
- He is a history buff with a compulsive urge for collecting videotapes and books about World War II and Adolf Hitler.
- He loves to travel, frequently visiting historic landmarks and museums, and has traveled widely in France, Ireland, the United Kingdom, Spain, and Canada.
- He is said to always carry a knife.

Bulger, now 79, is known to disguise himself by dying his hair, wearing a moustache, and donning different glasses. He is said to be proud of the three-year stretch he did at Alcatraz (for bank robbery), and, noted Teahan, "he has vowed that he will never, ever go back to prison."

Born and raised in the predominantly Irish-Catholic projects of South Boston, Bulger was involved in serious crimes at an early age, including assault, robbery, and rape.

After a stint in the Air Force and at several federal penitentiaries, he joined the Winter Hill Gang, which took over the South Boston crime scene. In addition to the murders he is charged with, he participated in drug trafficking, extortion, and loan-sharking, Teahan said.

Bulger's criminal enterprises over the last several decades may have earned him anywhere from $10 million to $30 million. He also infiltrated government agencies, including the FBI, sowing seeds of public distrust in law enforcement that remain in South Boston to this day. "He left a scar on the community," Teahan said, that will only be fully healed when he has been captured.

Despite the difficulty of the search, we have made some progress. For example, we have discovered two of Bulger's bank accounts. At Barclay's Bank in London, we found $75,000 in cash. At another of his accounts in Ireland, we found different types of currencies and rare coins.

Our multi-agency task force dedicated solely to finding Bulger (and his companion, Catherine Greig, who is under indictment for harboring a fugitive) continues to gather and analyze intelligence and respond to tips of sightings. The task force is made up of personnel from the FBI, the Massachusetts Department of Correction, and the Massachusetts State Police.

"We're committed to finding him," Teahan said. "No matter how long it takes."

We need your help. If you have any information on Bulger's whereabouts, contact your local FBI office or the nearest U.S. Embassy or Consulate.

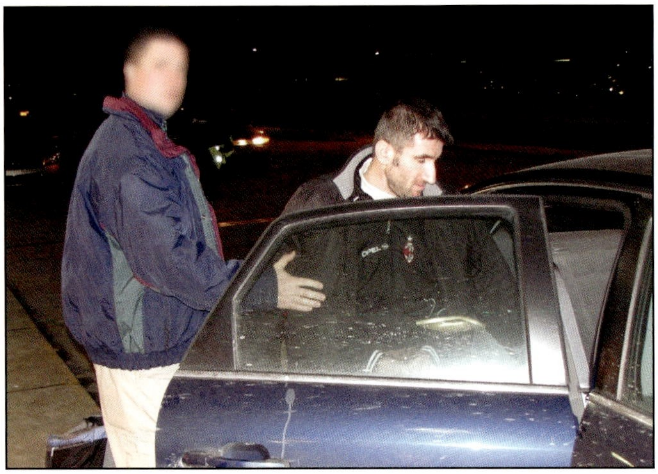

Left: A Detroit FBI agent puts Albanian criminal Drini Brahimllari into a car after his February 2008 return to the U.S. to face racketeering charges in Michigan.

MOVE OVER, MAFIA

The New Face of Organized Crime

When you hear the words "organized crime," the first thing that comes to mind is probably the Mafia and its five major crime families in New York City.

But have you ever heard of the notorious Thief-in-Law Vyacheslav Ivankov, the Solnstsevo organization, the Young Joon Yang gang, or the Black Dragons?

They're involved in organized crime, too. Individuals associated with foreign-based criminal groups are targeting the U.S. as we speak, and they are a major focus of American law enforcement and a top priority of the FBI's organized crime busting efforts.

These groups have much in common with the Mafia, beginning with their hunger for power and profit.

But what sets them apart is their reach. While traditional mobsters mostly operate domestically, Eurasian and Asian crime groups are transnational. Some report to an established leadership hierarchy in their native lands while others have fuzzier connections, but all require that we work closely with our global law enforcement partners.

Who they are. Eurasian criminal groups hail from dozens of countries spanning the Baltics, the Balkans, Central/Eastern Europe, Russia, the Caucasus, and Central Asia. Although ethnically-based, they work with other ethnic groups when perpetrating crimes. Asian organized crime includes traditional enterprises like the Chinese Triads, Chinese Tong, and Japanese Boryokudan (a.k.a., Yakuza), as well as more loosely organized groups like the Big Boys Circle, the Asian Boyz Group, and Vietnamese and Korean criminal enterprises.

What they do. Both groups are involved in a range of illegal activities in this country, including drug trafficking, extortion, murder, kidnapping, home invasions, prostitution, illegal gambling, loan sharking, insurance/credit card fraud, stock fraud, and the theft of high-tech components. Chinese groups are also involved in human trafficking—bringing large numbers of Chinese migrants to North America and essentially enslaving them here. One of U.S. law enforcement's chief concerns: the same criminal infrastructure that smuggles people into the U.S. could also be used to smuggle terrorists.

Investigative strategies. Over the past few decades, U.S. law enforcement has had a great deal of success against the major Mafia families using a full suite of investigative methods. Now, we're using the same set of tools to combat Eurasian and Asian crime groups, including:

- Intelligence gathering;
- The enterprise theory of investigation, which focuses on the entire criminal group rather than on isolated members;
- The Racketeer Influenced and Corrupt Organizations, or RICO, Act (both the criminal and civil provisions of this law can help dismantle criminal organizations);
- Cooperation, lots of it, with both domestic and global law enforcement partners; and
- Time-tested techniques like undercover operations, court-authorized electronic surveillance, and informants and cooperating witnesses.

Investigative accomplishments. Thief-in-Law Vyacheslav Ivankov's conviction in New York in 1996 represented the FBI's first major victory against the new wave of Eurasian organized crime entering America. Subsequent successes included Operation "Trojan Horses," which dismantled a violent New York City Albanian criminal enterprise that had taken traditional racketeering activity away from the established La Cosa Nostra crime families.

And undercover investigations in Newark and Los Angeles uncovered an Asian criminal organization that was smuggling, or attempting to smuggle, nearly every form of contraband imaginable—counterfeit currency, cigarettes, illegal drugs, pharmaceuticals, and weapons—into the United States.

FBI RECRUITERS

Looking to Our Future

"The FBI is only as good as its employees—and my job lets me play a part in choosing quality people to lead us into the future."

So says Jeffrey Westcott, an FBI agent from our Jacksonville office and a member of a team of recruiters who work out of our field offices around the country, looking for the best and brightest candidates to join us.

Our recruiters are diverse. They come from different ethnic backgrounds. Their academic backgrounds cover a wide range of fields. Some have a few years of FBI experience, while others have 20-plus.

But all have one thing in common: a commitment to hiring the next generation of employees. Special Agent Andrea Simmons from our El Paso office explains, "I know that I am a gatekeeper for the future of our organization—that's a huge responsibility that I take very seriously."

So why do they do it? Special Agent Manuel Johnson, Phoenix, explains that he became a recruiter because he "enjoys interacting with people who want to do what FBI employees do." Agent Westcott recalls being initially reluctant to become a recruiter, but "now four-plus years later, I'm still on the job, and I have no desire to do anything else." And Special Agent Juan Becerra, Salt Lake City, told us, "It's extremely rewarding go to out to colleges and universities talking about the FBI and seeing students get excited about a career with us."

What we look for in our recruiters. One of our human resources executives, Gwen Hubbard, says it's "an innate ability to relate to people, a passion about their work, and a sincere belief in our mission to protect this nation." Being an FBI recruiter, according to Hubbard, also requires working odd shifts, remaining connected to diverse organizations and cultures, and keeping up with the specifics of particular jobs within the FBI to make sure they're targeting the right people with the right skill sets.

FBI recruiters spend a large part of their day helping candidates through the application process, attending recruiting events, making appearances at schools, speaking before community groups...all in an effort to ensure that they have a high quality and diverse pool of candidates.

FBI Agent Jeffery Artis, a recruiter from our Jackson office, talks about opportunities in the Bureau with a potential applicant during a career fair at the University of Southern Mississippi.

The most common reasons applicants give for wanting to work at the FBI. A desire to serve the public is definitely the top answer. Special Agent Kal Wong, Honolulu, says it's all about "believing in public service and having the opportunity to work in an organization that promotes the welfare of our communities and our nation." Another reason is the variety of jobs. Explains Agent Simmons, "We offer so many great areas to work in—white-collar crime, terrorism, gangs, etc.—that you can have several mini-careers within one larger career."

Memorable candidates over the years. There are plenty, but two stand out in the minds of our recruiters: an attorney (and former U.S. Army captain) who gave up a six-figure salary to become a special agent; and a 69-year-old CPA who said he wanted to put his skills to work for the FBI rather than retire—and then went on to serve as a counterterrorism financial analyst.

Left: FBI Director Robert Mueller speaks about the changing face of international terrorism and the implications for our national security.

FROM MUMBAI TO SOMALIA

The Changing Landscape of Terror

Special Agent Steve Merrill joined the FBI to fight crime and to help make the world a safer place. But on one particular day last November, he was looking forward to his first day off in nearly a month. An Assistant Legal Attaché in our New Delhi office, Agent Merrill was on his way to play in a cricket tournament when he learned of the unfolding terrorist attack in Mumbai. Suddenly, cricket was the last thing on his mind.

Terrorists had landed on the shoreline of India's largest city at sundown, armed with automatic weapons and hand grenades. Within hours, buildings were ablaze and civilians were dead. During the three-day siege, more than 170 people were killed and 300 wounded.

Merrill was our first agent on the scene. Amid gunfire and explosions, he established lines of communication with his Indian and intelligence community counterparts, coordinated the arrival of our Rapid Deployment Team, and helped rescue trapped Americans inside the Taj Hotel.

The story of Agent Merrill's efforts—and our role in the Mumbai investigation—was told by Director Robert Mueller on Monday during a speech at the Council on Foreign Relations in Washington. His remarks offer a snapshot of today's FBI at work: internationally-based, intelligence-driven, fighting an endlessly changing and challenging universe of threats. One day we're dealing with a brazen terror attack across the ocean; the next—as the Director also discussed—we're sending our community outreach experts across the country to talk with immigrant families whose sons may be enticed to return to their homeland of Somalia to join the cause of violent extremists.

In Mumbai, our investigation began even before the crisis ended. Indian authorities gave us and our U.S. and international law enforcement partners unprecedented access to evidence and intelligence. We examined the scenes of several attacks. We conducted more than 60 interviews, including that of the lone surviving attacker. Our forensic specialists pulled fingerprints from improvised explosive devices and recovered data from damaged cell phones—in one case by literally wiring a smashed phone back together.

"This type of attack reminds us that terrorists with large agendas and little money can use rudimentary weapons to maximize their impact," Mueller said.

We counter today's terrorist threat by gathering intelligence and by using our proven investigative methods—the development of sources, surveillance, communication intercepts, and forensic analysis. This makes the Bureau not merely a law enforcement organization, Mueller pointed out, but also "a security service, fusing the capability to understand the breadth and scope of threats with the capability to dismantle them."

Another aspect of our proactive approach to fighting terrorism is our community outreach program. Case in point: our ongoing partnership with civic and religious leaders in the Somali-American community.

It has been widely reported by the media that young men from Minneapolis may be traveling to Somalia to join extremists fighting for control of the country. The Director indicated that a man who appears to have been radicalized in Minneapolis "became what we believe to be the first U.S. citizen to carry out a terrorist suicide bombing" after launching an attack last October in northern Somalia. Our outreach teams "meet with members of these communities to look at these issues," Mueller said. "Together, we are making progress."

MURDER ON THE HIGH SEAS

The Strange, Sad Tale of *Joe Cool*

On a warm Saturday afternoon in September, a fishing boat named the *Joe Cool* set sail from the port of Miami. Its destination: the beautiful island of Bimini in the Bahamas.

On board were four crew members—a husband-wife team, one of their relatives, and a good friend—along with two men who'd chartered the vessel to visit their girlfriends.

What the crew didn't know was that this was no ordinary charter cruise. One of the passengers, Kirby Logan Archer, was on the run from the law. And there were no girlfriends waiting in the Bahamas. Only trouble—and tragedy—lay ahead.

The following evening, when the boat didn't return to port as scheduled and the crew could not be contacted, worried family members called the Coast Guard.

On Monday morning, when agents from our Maritime Seaport Squad were called in, the facts were still hazy, but one thing was becoming clear: a gruesome crime had been committed at sea. There was blood on the deck. All four crew members were missing. And the two passengers—Archer and another man named Guillermo Zarabozo—were soon found adrift in a life raft, telling a wild story about how the boat had been attacked by Cuban pirates.

We took the lead in the investigation, based on federal law regarding crimes on the high seas. After getting the call from the Coast Guard on Monday, September 24, 2007, Special Agents David Nunez and Herbert "Skip" Hogberg in our Miami office knew they had to act fast. It would take a day or more to tow the recovered 47-foot fishing boat back to Miami, and all the exposed evidence would be subjected to the elements—wind, rain, and sea spray that would wash away blood, fibers, fingerprints, and more.

So Nunez, other agents, and representatives of the Coast Guard boarded a jet to the Florida Keys, hopped on a helicopter to a Coast Guard cutter, and from there took a "fast boat" to the deserted *Joe Cool*, which was about 30 miles from Cuba. They quickly collected and preserved the evidence and interviewed Archer and Zarabozo after they were picked up from the raft.

The 47-foot charter fishing boat *Joe Cool*

Investigators soon realized that the men had planned all along to hijack the boat to Cuba, where Archer hoped to escape the U.S. legal system. He was being investigated in Arkansas for child molestation and was charged with robbing a Wal-Mart of $92,000. Investigators believe Archer duped Zarabozo—described as a "CIA-wannabe"—into thinking he was joining a CIA mission to Cuba.

The pirate story never held up, least of all because credit cards, electronics, and $70,000 worth of fishing gear had been left behind on the *Joe Cool*. "Pirates would have taken all of that," Hogberg said.

With their story in tatters and evidence mounting against them, Archer accepted a plea of life in prison rather than face the death penalty at trial. Zarabozo maintained that he took no part in the murders, but a Miami jury last week didn't buy it and returned guilty verdicts on all counts.

In the end, nothing about Archer's plan worked. After the murders, the boat had run out of gas, and he and Zarabozo were forced into the raft, with nothing to do but wait for justice to arrive. And it surely did.

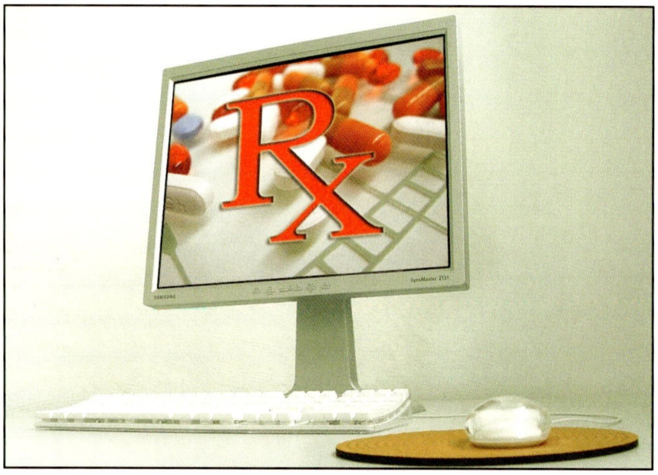

DON'T PUT YOUR HEALTH

In the Hands of Crooks

It couldn't be easier—ordering prescription drugs online with a few clicks of the mouse and having them delivered right to your door, without ever having to see a doctor.

But is it safe? Is it legal?

Often not. And you need to know the risks.

Yes, there are plenty of legitimate U.S. pharmaceutical companies and pharmacies (including online ones) that follow all the laws and regulations and put public safety first.

But there are many that don't—they are just out to make a fast buck at your expense. These shady businesses fill orders without prescriptions. They pay doctors just to take a quick glance at your brief medical questionnaire. They don't know if you are drug-addicted, underage, or have another condition that their medications could make worse. And they don't care.

Worse yet, the products they peddle are questionable, at best. The drugs may be way past their expiration date. They may be counterfeit, mislabeled, adulterated, or contaminated. And they may well be made from suspect raw materials in underground laboratories in the U.S. and abroad, far from the safety-conscious eyes of the Food and Drug Administration.

Part of the problem is that these illegal pharmacies are all over the Internet. More than 80,000 "portal" websites currently sell ad space for these medications and link to one of more than 1,400 "anchor" websites that allow customers to place orders through illegal pharmacies. You don't even have to search for these offers—they often come straight to your inbox as e-mail spam, enticing you with a cornucopia of drugs on the cheap.

Are there ways to tell whether an online pharmacy is legal? Definitely, and here's what to look for. Legitimate pharmacies:

- Require a prescription from a licensed doctor, usually by mail (if they accept a fax copy, they will always call your doctor to verify the prescription);
- Make you submit a detailed medical history;
- Clearly state their payment, privacy, and shipping fees on their sites; and
- Use secure or encrypted website connections for transactions.

Many legitimate online pharmacies are also certified by the National Association of Boards of Pharmacy—check its website for a listing. Bear in mind, some of the larger Internet pharmacies may not be certified because of their already well-recognized names.

To help protect you, the FBI has made Internet pharmacy fraud one of its top health care fraud priorities. We work—and train—with federal investigators from our partner agencies. We also work closely with state and local law enforcement, and, because many illegal online pharmacies have global connections, we often coordinate with our overseas partners.

Just one example of a major crackdown: in August 2007, a San Diego grand jury handed down a 313-count indictment against 18 people, charging them with operating an illegal online pharmacy that netted more than **$126 million** over a two-year period. Incredibly, this network—which included everyone from doctors and druggists to credit card processors and affiliated websites that advertised the illegal wares—allegedly received over a million Internet orders from customers in all 50 states.

Our bottom-line advice: do your homework and steer clear of illegal Internet pharmacies, even if the prices are tempting. It's your health, after all.

DILLINGER CROSSES A LINE

The Year of the Gangster, Part 1

An elderly janitor walked into the cell block of the Lake County Jail at Crown Point, Indiana. The date: March 3, 1934. It was a relatively new facility, built onto the back of the sheriff's house in 1926, easy to clean, impossible to escape from. The addition of a notorious prisoner—John Dillinger—would prove that. Or so the sheriff thought.

As the janitor entered the cell, the prisoner jumped him and jammed a gun—actually a piece of wood carved in the shape of one—into his ribs. Quickly, through a combination of bravado and desperation, Dillinger tricked half a dozen guards back to the cell block, confiscated their weapons, and jailed the jailors.

On that day, Dillinger was 30 years old. He was of medium build and average height, with brown, thinning hair. His most distinguishing feature was a roguish smile, which he had put to good use in a series of press photos with the prosecuting attorney Robert Estill and the sheriff upon his extradition to Crown Point. The chummy nature of the photos contributed to both these officials losing their jobs that year. And Dillinger's charm had already begun to captivate the American people, who began to see him as part Robin Hood, part vicious thug.

The notorious gangster had been captured in Arizona two months earlier. He was wanted in connection with the murder of an East Chicago, Indiana police officer named William O'Malley. At the time Dillinger was not on our radar; he had committed no federal crimes. But we had been assisting Ohio law enforcement in their search for him after was freed from a Lima jail by his confederates in the fall of 1933.

Now Dillinger had escaped once more. In making the break, he'd stolen the sheriff's car and driven it to Chicago, 50 or so miles northwest of Crown Point. In the process, he crossed the Indiana/Illinois border and violated the National Motor Vehicle Theft Act, commonly called the "Dyer Act." John Dillinger was now a federal fugitive and an FBI subject.

Over the next several months, the Bureau tracked Dillinger and a wide array of violent criminals who worked with him—making mistakes along the way, but ultimately bringing these violent criminals to justice.

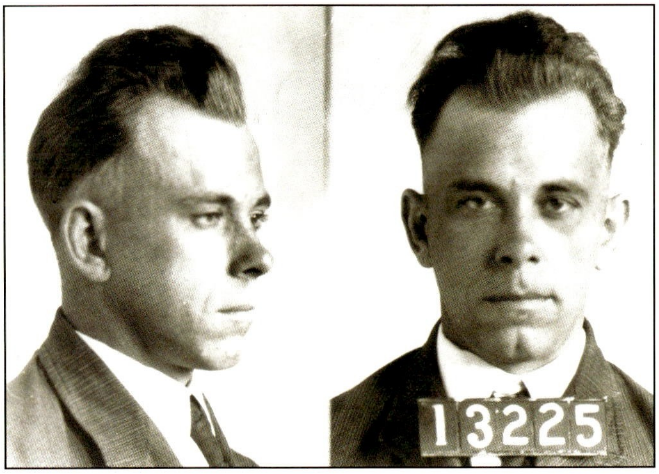

Photos from an early Dillinger wanted flyer

This year marks the 75th anniversary of that chase. More importantly, it is the 75th anniversary of the emergence of the FBI as an organization of national and international stature.

The Bureau's success in dealing with the gangsters led to significant changes in the FBI and law enforcement nationwide. Over the next few months, we will spotlight what we are calling "The Year of the Gangster" on our website through stories, photographs, and multimedia presentations, along with some new case details. We will tell how we went after such desperados as Bonnie and Clyde, "Pretty Boy" Floyd, "Baby Face" Nelson, and more. We will examine the social and political changes that arose from these criminal threats, bring to light long-forgotten historical sources, and consider the role that the Gangster Era played in the evolution of the FBI and its portrayal in American popular culture.

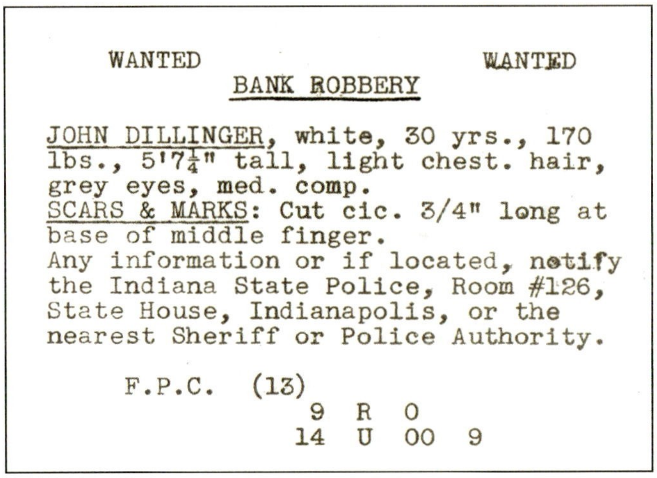

WANTED WANTED

BANK ROBBERY

JOHN DILLINGER, white, 30 yrs., 170 lbs., 5'7¼" tall, light chest. hair, grey eyes, med. comp.
SCARS & MARKS: Cut cic. 3/4" long at base of middle finger.
Any information or if located, notify the Indiana State Police, Room #126, State House, Indianapolis, or the nearest Sheriff or Police Authority.

F.P.C. (13)
9 R 0
14 U 00 9

Additional details from the wanted flyer

SEEKING VICTIMS

In the Stanford Financial Group Case

Have you invested in the Stanford Financial Group or its affiliated companies in recent years? If so, you may be a victim of a multi-billion dollar investment fraud.

The Stanford Financial Group, which provides wealth management services to customers in some 140 countries, is under FBI investigation. On February 26, its Chief Investment Officer was charged with obstructing a separate investigation by the U.S. Securities and Exchange Commission.

Our case is ongoing, and while we can't provide any additional information on our investigation at this time, we do need to hear from you to identify victims and to determine the extent of the potential fraud.

What we need to know:

- Your basic contact information (name, address, country, telephone numbers, e-mail address);
- Your investments/losses with Stanford Financial Group or its affiliated companies: Stanford Capital Management, the Stanford Group Company, the Stanford International Bank, the Stanford Trust Company, and the Bank of Antigua;
- Whether or not you can verify your investments/losses by providing your most recent financial statements; and
- Any additional information that may be helpful.

How to provide the above information:

- Submit via a dedicated e-mail address: stanford.group@ic.fbi.gov.

If you have *investigative* information that might help our case, please use our electronic public leads and tips form at https://tips.fbi.gov/.

Please send copies of any hard copy documentation to:

FBI Victim Assistance Program
Post Office Box 924427
Houston, TX 77292-4427

If we determine that you are a victim, we will be in touch with you. Please note: due to the number of expected responses, you may not hear back from us for several weeks.

Investors may also call (713) 693-5699 for recorded information on the victim assistance program. At this time we are unable to accept messages on this line because of expected call volume.

"The FBI understands the devastating financial, emotional, and physical impact that fraud can have in the lives of individuals and families," says Kathryn Turman, Director of our Office for Victim Assistance. "We see it every day. Even in these large-scale cases, the victims and their losses are not just numbers to us. Even when we cannot restore lost funds we can usually provide help, hope, and support as we also work to bring justice to the perpetrators who are suspected of inflicting the damage."

March 12, 2009

FUSION CENTERS

Unifying Intelligence to Protect Americans

In Arizona, after determining the subjects of an international terrorism case were involved in local criminal activity, the case was referred to local law enforcement. In New Mexico, several individuals linked to FBI investigations—including an MS-13 gang member—were identified. In Tennessee, we developed—with our partners—a formal process for collecting, sharing, and analyzing suspicious activity reports, looking for trends and patterns.

These cooperative efforts—and many more like them—have been made possible through the work of intelligence fusion centers around the country. These centers, usually set up by states or major urban areas and run by state or local authorities, are often supported by federal law enforcement, including the FBI.

This week, nearly 2,000 local, state, tribal, and federal representatives working in these centers gathered in Kansas City to continue the process of standardizing fusion center operations. The ultimate goal? To create a network of centers presenting a unified front against terrorism and other national security and criminal threats that put Americans at risk.

Speaking at the Kansas City conference, our Chief Intel Officer Don Van Duyn said that "while we still have work to do to make the information process more seamless," the FBI is committed to "expanding our interconnectedness" to help combat threats from terrorist and criminal networks. He also said that during the past year we have rolled out—to all of our 56 field offices—standardized intelligence operations structures, roles, and procedures to enhance our collaboration with our partners.

Although a few were already in existence before 9/11, fusion centers really began to crop up after the attacks when local and federal officials recognized the need to quickly coordinate information-sharing related to terrorism. Their number has been growing ever since. Today, there are some 70 centers around the country—50 state and 20 regional. And some have expanded their focus to include public safety matters and major criminal threats.

Fusion center personnel "fuse" intelligence from participating agencies to create a more comprehensive threat picture, locally and nationally. They don't just collect information—they integrate new data into existing information, evaluate it to determine its worth, analyze it for links and trends, and disseminate their findings to the agency in the best position to do something about it.

Inside the Arizona Counter Terrorism Information Center, the state's fusion center.

FBI representation. We currently have 114 FBI employees working in 38 fusion centers—about 36 percent are agents, 61 percent are intelligence analysts, and the rest are in positions such as language and financial analysts. Fourteen of these centers are co-located with an FBI Field Intelligence Group or Joint Terrorism Task Force.

Says Elaine Cummins, our Chief Information Sharing Officer, "Participating in a national network of fusion centers definitely helps us share timely, relevant, and actionable intelligence with our partners—an increasingly important component to our unique national security and law enforcement mission."

With fusion centers, everbody wins. State and local law enforcement agencies get access to certain federal databases and the benefit of big-picture terrorism and crime perspectives from their federal partners, along with grant funding, technical assistance, and training. Federal agencies like the FBI gain intelligence from the local level that may fuel terrorism or national security investigations elsewhere in the country or even overseas.

And the public gets to sleep a little easier at night, knowing that their local, state, and federal officials are all working **together** to keep them safe.

March 17, 2009

Left: Did the famous hijacker take his name from a popular comic book hero? © Dan Cooper – Albert Weinberg – Le Lombard (Dargaud-Lombard s.a.) – 2009.

IN SEARCH OF D.B. COOPER

New Developments in the Unsolved Case

Electron microscopes, dollar bills on a fishing pole, and a French Canadian comic book hero are providing tantalizing new insights into one of our greatest unsolved mysteries—the D.B. Cooper case.

We've told the story here before—how in 1971 a man calling himself Dan Cooper hijacked a plane from Portland to Seattle, demanded parachutes and $200,000 in cash, then jumped into the night with the money, never to be seen again.

Did he survive the jump? That is the subject of great debate. But as it turns out, a certain Dan Cooper is very much alive—on the pages of a French comic book series that was popular when the hijacking occurred. In the fictional series, Royal Canadian Air Force test pilot Dan Cooper takes part in adventures in outer space and real events of that era. In one episode, published near the date of the hijacking, the cover illustration shows him parachuting.

Seattle Special Agent Larry Carr, who took over the Cooper case two years ago, believes it's possible the hijacker took his name from the comic book (the enduring "D.B." was actually the result of a media mistake). That's important because the books were never translated into English, which means the hijacker likely spent time overseas. This fits with Carr's theory that Cooper had been in the Air Force.

Carr discovered the comic book connection on D.B. Cooper Internet forums, where fascination with the case is undiminished. The forums are also where Carr found the "citizen sleuths" who volunteered to help us reinvigorate the case.

Special Agent Larry Carr

Even though our investigation has remained open, it doesn't make sense for the FBI to commit substantial resources to this nearly four-decade-old crime, Carr says. "So if the public can help, by whatever means, maybe we can shake something loose."

Enter Tom Kaye, a paleontologist who usually searches for dinosaur bones in the Wyoming desert. With a team that included a scientific illustrator and a metallurgist, and assistance from a veteran Cooper searcher and Brian Ingram—who was eight years old in 1980 when he found $5,800 of the ransom money on a sand bar along the Columbia River (the only physical evidence in the case after Cooper jumped from the plane)—Kaye recently spent time conducting soil, water, and other experiments on the Columbia and some of its tributaries.

"The FBI threw out the challenge," he said, "and we've taken the bait."

Using technology unavailable in 1971, such as satellite maps and GPS, Kaye hopes to pinpoint exactly where Ingram found the money nearly three decades ago. He plans to retrace the plane's flight plan to determine more exact coordinates for Cooper's landing zone. And using an electron microscope, he wants to figure out if pollen found on a tie Cooper left behind on the plane came from a specific region of the country.

And that stack of dollar bills on fishing line? Kaye conducted experiments to help determine if the money Ingram found floated there over time or was buried there shortly after Cooper jumped. "After 37 years," he said, "we're trying to use science to narrow all the possibilities."

It's yet another twist in a case that continues to fascinate the nation.

If you have any information on Cooper, please e-mail our Seattle field office at Seattle.FBI@ic.fbi.gov.

DIFFERENCE MAKERS

Heroes in Our Communities

A high school teacher who spends his afternoons and weekends counseling at-risk kids. A family that turned personal tragedy into an outpouring of hope and healing for others. A Hollywood actor who has become a tireless advocate for children.

Today, in a first-of-its-kind ceremony at our national Headquarters in Washington, D.C., we paid tribute to more than 50 civic leaders and humanitarian-minded organizations from across the country. Each is a 2008 winner of our Director's Community Leadership Award, which since 1990 has celebrated those who have made significant contributions to public wellbeing and security. The award is presented annually by the Special Agents in Charge in all of our 56 field offices and by our Community Relations team at FBI Headquarters.

This year's winners are a special group. They have worked to combat such scourges as child abuse, domestic violence, gangs and drugs, violent crime, illiteracy, and racial and religious prejudice. They have championed such causes as interfaith dialogue and global compassion. They have tended to the needs of at-risk youth, immigrants and refugees, and the families of fallen firefighters and law enforcement officers.

The honorees come from all walks of life. They include a mayor and a pastor, an imam and an investigative reporter, a pediatrician and a former professional football player. Many have worked with us directly—to investigate and prevent crime and terrorism, to raise awareness about our mission, to build new and stronger relationships with all segments of society, or to publicize wanted fugitives and missing persons.

We have posted on our website a list of the winners and their achievements—along with a high-resolution photograph of each attendee with FBI Director Robert Mueller.

Here are just a few of their inspiring stories:

- **Memphis, Tennessee:** Dr. Mohammed Moinuddin has dedicated himself to helping local Muslim refugees and to improving relationships among Jewish, Christian, Hindu, and Muslim communities. Why does he do it? He asks: "Don't we all want a better, more peaceful city to live in…with a better understanding between people of different faiths, ethnicities, and backgrounds?"

Director Robert S. Mueller congratulates representatives of four of the nation's largest billboard companies—Clear Channel Outdoor, Adams Outdoor Advertising, Lamar Advertising, and the Outdoor Advertising Association of Georgia. In little more than a year, their efforts in our Digital Billboard initiative have been instrumental in apprehending 18 people sought by authorities.

- **Albany, New York:** After a 10-year-old girl was struck down by a stray bullet, Pastor Charles Muller channeled his anger and frustration into a highly successful gun buy-back program to help keep weapons off the street. His said his choice was easy: "We could either turn our head and have a deaf ear…or do something about it."
- **Sacramento, California:** On the job, Assistant U.S. Attorney Laurel White of the Eastern District of California has seen it all while prosecuting online child predators. She also spends much of her free time warning her community about the dangers lurking on the Internet. She said her mission is to "educate parents and their kids…and work with schools to help them implement Internet safety curriculums of their own…to prevent these crimes from ever occurring in the first place."
- **El Paso, Texas:** Susan Oliva—Director of the Advocacy Center for the Children of El Paso—has worked to create a "safe place where children victimized by severe physical or sexual abuse could be given the opportunity to be heard and to heal."

Congratulations to all the award winners—we are proud to call you our partners.

Left: In Tampa, some of the luxury vehicles seized in "Operation Duel Identity," a multiagency investigation into car cloning and auto theft that spanned 20 states and three countries.

STEERING CLEAR OF CAR CLONING

Some Advice and Solutions

Car cloning: stealing the identity of a legitimately-owned vehicle and slapping it onto a stolen car.

It's a serious crime problem that's being aggressively investigated by law enforcement. For example: today in Tampa, we joined with our partners in announcing that 17 major players in a long-running car cloning criminal enterprise have been indicted by a federal grand jury.

The good news is that in the not-too-distance future, a new national database may help make car cloning a thing of the past.

How does car cloning work? Like the Tampa case, it begins with a stolen vehicle—usually a luxury car or fully-loaded SUV.

Then, the vehicle is "cloned"—its manufacturer-installed Vehicle Identification Number (VIN) plate is pried off and replaced with another one. This second VIN plate actually holds a legitimate number that came from a vehicle of a similar make and model in a different state. Other phony ownership documents complete the cloning. At that point it can be easily registered with a motor vehicle agency in another state.

Once the stolen vehicle is registered anew, it can be sold. In the Tampa case, more than 1,000 cloned cars were sold to witting and unwitting buyers in 20 states and several countries, with estimated losses of more than $25 million to consumers, auto insurers, and other victims.

So how big is the possible impact of cloning on consumers? Huge. If you buy a cloned vehicle and its true pedigree is discovered, the car will be confiscated, and you'll still be responsible for any outstanding loans. If your vehicle is the victim of car cloning, you could be accused of a variety of offenses—from parking tickets or cutting somebody off in traffic...to serious criminal activity like organized crime. And you could spend a great deal of time and money trying to prove that it wasn't you or your car after all.

Enter NMVTIS, or the National Motor Vehicle Title Information System. This Department of Justice database, operated by the American Association of Motor Vehicle Administrators, is an electronic system that links state motor vehicle departments together...and once fully operational should go a long way towards shutting down car cloning activities. If a car is titled in one state, a criminal should not be able to steal its VIN and use it on another vehicle in another state—the database will spit out a hit showing that the number is already in use.

So far, 37 states participate or are in the process of participating in the system. A federal law mandated the creation of the database and the participation of all 50 states by next year.

Tips on how to steer clear of car cloning:

- If you think your car was cloned (for instance, you receive notice of unpaid parking tickets that aren't yours), contact your local police.
- If you're car shopping, beware of a car being sold for substantially less than comparable makes and models.
- Get a copy of the car's vehicle history report.
- Check out the VIN plate on the dashboard for any evidence of tampering (scratches, etc.).
- Look for incorrect spellings on paperwork, like vehicle titles.
- Trust your intuition—if it sounds too good to be true, it probably is!

INTERNET CRIME
Complaints and Losses on the Rise

Reports of Internet scams and their financial toll continued to grow in 2008, according to the latest data by the Internet Crime Complaint Center (IC3), which operates a website, www.ic3.gov, to collect and refer public complaints about Internet fraud.

In 2008, more than $264 million was lost in 275,284 complaints—an average of $931 for every complaint—according to the 2008 Internet Crime Report, released March 30. Almost one-third of the complaints were for non-delivery of merchandise purchased online; auction fraud accounted for one in four complaints.

In one case cited in the 2008 figures, a Virginia woman—Rachel Trent, who was the subject of multiple complaints in three states—advertised rare baseball and football cards on the eBay auction site. Once a buyer paid, the woman sent a worthless card or sometimes nothing at all. She was arrested by a cyber task force and is serving fours years in prison.

The Internet Crime Complaint Center is a partnership between the FBI and the nonprofit National White Collar Crime Center. IC3 collects the data, analyzes it, and then refers complaints to law enforcement agencies to follow up. The report, issued annually since 2003, offers a snapshot of the most frequent Internet crimes, where they are occurring, and who is being victimized.

In the U.S. last year, California, New York, Florida, Texas, and the District of Columbia were home to half the perpetrators identified in complaints. Worldwide, perpetrators were most commonly from the U.S. (66.1 percent), followed by the United Kingdom (10.5 percent), Nigeria (7.5 percent), and Canada (3.1 percent).

Here's a look at the scams prompting the most complaints (by percentage), along with the average amount of money lost per complaint:

- Non-delivery of merchandise/payment: $800 (32.9 percent)
- Auction fraud: $610 (25.5 percent)
- Credit/debit card fraud: $223 (9 percent)
- Confidence fraud: $2,000 (7.9 percent)
- Computer fraud: $1,000 (6.2 percent)

- Check fraud: $3,000 (5.4 percent)
- Nigerian letter fraud: $1,650 (2.8 percent)

The data is posted in full on the IC3 website.

"This report illustrates that sophisticated computer fraud schemes continue to flourish as financial data migrates to the Internet," FBI Cyber Division Assistant Director Shawn Henry said in a statement.

Year	Complaints	Loss
2008	275,284	$265 million
2007	206,884	$239 million
2006	207,492	$198 million
2005	231,493	$183 million
2004	207,449	$68 million

The 2008 figures represent a 33 percent increase in complaints and a $25 million increase in losses over 2007. E-mail and webpages were the two primary mechanisms scammers used to commit their crimes, underscoring the need to be vigilant and cautious online, particularly in transactions. The Internet Crime Report offers prevention tips to avoid online traps. You can also visit our Be Crime Smart webpage to learn about frauds, scams, and how to file tips and complaints.

SPEAR PHISHERS

Angling to Steal Your Financial Info

Customers of a telecommunications firm received an e-mail recently explaining a problem with their latest order. They were asked to go to the company website, via a link in the e-mail, to provide personal information—like their birthdates and Social Security numbers. But both the e-mail and the website were bogus.

It's a real-life, classic case of "phishing"—a virtual trap set by cyber thieves that uses official-looking e-mails to lure you to fake websites and trick you into revealing your personal information.

It's also an example of an even more mischievous type of phishing known as "spear phishing"—a rising cyber threat that you need to know about.

Instead of casting out thousands of e-mails randomly hoping a few victims will bite, spear phishers target select groups of people with something in common—they work at the same company, bank at the same financial institution, attend the same college, order merchandise from the same website, etc. The e-mails are ostensibly sent from organizations or individuals the potential victims would normally get e-mails from, making them even more deceptive.

How spear phishing works. First, criminals need *some* inside information on their targets to convince them the e-mails are legitimate. They often obtain it by hacking into an organization's computer network (which is what happened in the above case) or sometimes by combing through other websites, blogs, and social networking sites.

Then, they send e-mails that look like the real thing to targeted victims, offering all sorts of urgent and legitimate-sounding explanations as to why they need your personal data.

Finally, the victims are asked to click on a link inside the e-mail that takes them to a phony but realistic-looking website, where they are asked to provide passwords, account numbers, user IDs, access codes, PINs, etc.

Criminal gain, your loss. Once criminals have your personal data, they can access your bank account, use your credit cards, and create a whole new identity using your information.

Spear phishing can also trick you into downloading malicious codes or malware after you click on a link embedded in the e-mail...an especially useful tool in crimes like economic espionage where sensitive internal communications can be accessed and trade secrets stolen. Malware can also hijack your computer, and hijacked computers can be organized into enormous networks called botnets that can be used for denial of service attacks.

How to avoid becoming a spear phishing victim. Law enforcement takes this kind of crime seriously, and we in the FBI work cyber investigations with our partners, including the U.S. Secret Service and investigative agencies within the Department of Defense. But what can you do to make sure you don't end up a victim in one of our cases?

- Keep in mind that most companies, banks, agencies, etc., don't request personal information via e-mail. If in doubt, give them a call (but don't use the phone number contained in the e-mail—that's usually phony as well).
- Use a phishing filter...many of the latest web browsers have them built in or offer them as plug-ins.
- Never follow a link to a secure site from an e-mail—always enter the URL manually.
- Don't be fooled (especially today) by the latest scams. Visit the Internet Crime Complaint Center (IC3) and "LooksTooGoodToBeTrue" websites for tips and information.

COLD CASE HEATS UP

Help Solve 1988 Murder, Part 1

The innocent face of 8-year-old April Tinsley is projected from a large screen in front of the conference room as about 50 law enforcement officials—including a special team from the FBI—begin their meeting.

April's picture was a powerful reminder of why the group had gathered: on Good Friday 21 years ago, the young girl was abducted from her neighborhood in Fort Wayne, Indiana and then raped and murdered. Her killer is still at large.

The meeting at the National Center for Missing & Exploited Children in Virginia took place because state and local Indiana law enforcement officers—who remain dedicated to solving the case—have asked for help from our Child Abduction Rapid Deployment Team, known as CARD.

CARD Teams were created three years ago to bring together a variety of experts in child abduction cases who could quickly respond on the ground to help local authorities with time-sensitive investigations.

Team members include:

- Personnel from our Behavioral Analysis Unit, who profile offenders' personality traits and possible motives;
- Agents and analysts from our Crimes Against Children Unit;
- Coordinators from the National Center for the Analysis of Violent Crime; and
- Representatives from the Violent Criminal Apprehension Program (VICAP).

CARD consists of 48 members organized into 10 teams in five regions around the country. Since the program's creation, teams have deployed 38 times and aided in the recovery of 18 children.

As the name suggests, CARD Teams respond rapidly in cases of non-family abductions, ransom abductions, and the mysterious disappearances of children. But CARD also works cold cases, such as the April Tinsley murder. And as team members discovered, there is enough evidence—including notes, pictures, and DNA left by the killer years after the murder—to make investigators hopeful they can break the case.

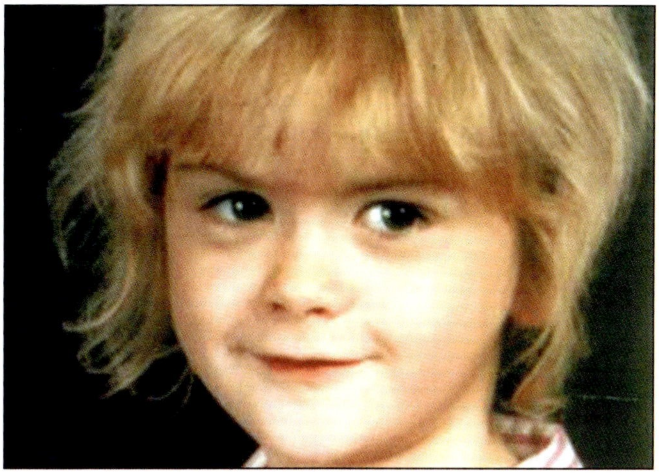

Eight-year-old April Tinsley was abducted, raped, and murdered on Good Friday in 1988.

It was a chilly Friday afternoon in 1988 when April was abducted walking home from a friend's house. Her body was found three days later about 20 miles away in a rural area dotted with Amish farms.

Despite an intensive search, police were unable to find her killer. Two years later, a message written in pencil or crayon appeared on a barn door not far from where April's body had been discovered. The writer claimed responsibility for the murder.

Then, in the spring of 2004, four notes appeared at various residences in the Fort Wayne area—several placed on bicycles that young girls had left in their yards—believed to be written by the killer. The notes, all on lined yellow paper, were placed inside baggies along with used condoms or Polaroid pictures of the killer's body. Several of the notes referred to April Tinsley.

Since those 2004 notes, the killer has not been heard from. But he has left a trail of evidence that the CARD Team hopes to exploit during its deployment to Fort Wayne, tentatively scheduled for later this spring. Investigators believe the case is "highly solvable," and after 21 years, their desire to bring April Tinsley's killer to justice is stronger than ever.

We need your help. Contact your local FBI office or the Fort Wayne Police Department if you have any information.

HIGHWAY SERIAL KILLINGS

New Initiative on an Emerging Trend

In 2004, an analyst from the Oklahoma Bureau of Investigation detected a crime pattern: the bodies of murdered women were being dumped along the Interstate 40 corridor in Oklahoma, Texas, Arkansas, and Mississippi.

The analyst and a police colleague from the Grapevine, Texas Police Department referred these cases to our Violent Criminal Apprehension Program, or ViCAP, where our analysts looked at other records in our database to see if there were similar patterns of highway killings elsewhere.

Turns out there were. So we launched an extensive effort to support our state and local partners with open investigations into highway murders.

Today, we're publicly announcing our Highway Serial Killings initiative to raise awareness among law enforcement agencies and the general public about this issue and our unique assistance on these cases.

First, some background. The victims in these cases are primarily women who are living high-risk, transient lifestyles, often involving substance abuse and prostitution. They're frequently picked up at truck stops or service stations and sexually assaulted, murdered, and dumped along a highway.

The suspects are predominantly long-haul truck drivers. But the mobile nature of the offenders, the unsafe lifestyles of the victims, the distances and multiple jurisdictions involved, and the scarcity of witnesses or forensic evidence can make these cases tough to solve.

Enter ViCAP, part of our National Center for the Analysis of Violent Crime and a national repository for violent crimes. The database—which contains information on homicides, sexual assaults, missing persons, and unidentified human remains—is available to law enforcement throughout the country over a secure Internet link on our Law Enforcement Online (LEO).

ViCAP analysts have created a national matrix of more than 500 murder victims from along or near highways, as well as a list of some 200 potential suspects. Names of suspects—contributed by law enforcement agencies—are examined by analysts who develop timelines using a variety of reliable sources of information.

Our assistance also includes:

- Sponsoring free regional training sessions on our Highway Serial Killings initiative for law enforcement agencies located near major interstates and highways;
- Educating victim advocacy groups, in particular groups representing women and children; and
- Using the skills of our behavioral analysis experts at the National Center for the Analysis of Violent Crime, who can provide investigative, interview, and prosecutive strategies; ways to link cases using behavioral characteristics; advice on working with the media; and unknown offender profiles.

ViCAP, though, is only as good as the data it contains, so we ask law enforcement agencies to make sure they submit to us their cases involving murders and other violent crimes taking place on or near highways.

Bottom line: Is the Highway Serial Killings initiative solving cases? Yes, it is. So far, at least 10 suspects believed responsible for some 30 homicides have been placed in custody…including a trucker arrested in Tennessee charged with four murders and a trucker charged with one murder in Massachusetts and another in New Jersey.

But what about the case that started it all—the series of murdered women being dumped along the Interstate 40 corridor in Oklahoma and three other states? Two people who were working together have been charged with some of the murders…and the investigation to tie them to others continues.

GETTING PHYSICAL
Our Hardcopy Forensic Experts

Today, it's forensic science 101. But back in the early 1930s, when Bruno Hauptmann left a series of ransom notes after snatching (and later killing) the Lindberghs' 20-month-old son, he probably never realized that painstaking analysis of his handwriting by the emerging FBI Laboratory would add to the volumes of evidence and help convict him of the sensational murder.

More than 75 years later—even in this digital age—our ever-expanding ability to glean clues from a whole range of physical documents and materials is essential to solving our cases and often those of our partners.

"We've worked just about every major case," said Diana Harrison, who heads what we call our Questioned Documents Unit (QDU) in the FBI Lab, "because every investigation has a paper trail."

The unit's 17 forensic document examiners, for instance, pored over charred documents after the 9/11 attacks to help identify the hijackers. They pieced together shredded documents in the Enron case, analyzed cryptic notes from Kansas serial killer Dennis Rader, and compared outsoles on size 12 Bruno Magli shoes as part of the O.J. Simpson murder investigation. The list goes on and on.

Babe Ruth's signature looks authentic, but examiners found that the ball's cork center design was too modern to be used during Ruth's era.

Known mainly for its handwriting analysis, the unit actually performs 25 different types of exams—all without tainting or destroying evidence. Its examiners are skilled in analyzing inks, papers, plastic bags, tire treads, and typewriters (still in use more than you might expect). The unit also maintains extensive databases of bank robbery notes, anonymous letters, shoe prints, and fake checks—quite handy when comparing and contrasting clues from across the nation.

The FBI Questioned Documents Unit may be best known for handwriting analysis.

A few more examples of the unit's capabilities:

- A single match left at the scene of an arson can be compared to a matchbook found on a suspect, and, based on analysis using a variety of equipment and techniques, examiners can often determine with a high degree of certainty if the match found at the scene came from the suspect's matchbook.
- Using a device called an Electrostatic Detection Apparatus, examiners can find indented, or "secret," writing that may be invisible to the naked eye. Pete Belcastro, a veteran QDU examiner, provides a real-life example: when a bank robber handed a teller a note demanding money, he didn't realize that it secretly gave away his identify. When he had earlier scribbled out his name and address on a pad of paper, it made an impression on the piece of paper below it, on which he later wrote his robbery note.

One of QDU's biggest cases was Operation Bullpen, a huge sports memorabilia and celebrity forgery ring that began in the mid-1990s. The crooks hired art students and gave them months to perfect the signatures of Mickey Mantle, Elvis Presley, and many others. The forgeries were "very, very close" to the authentic signatures, Belcastro said, but the bad guys hadn't thought of everything. In one case, a vintage-looking baseball with Babe Ruth's signature seemed like the real thing on the outside, but when examiners cut the ball in half, they found a cork center not used in the Bambino's era.

"We take a great deal of pride and satisfaction in the scientific work we do," Belcastro said. "And it's nice to know that what we do makes a difference."

Left: John Zagelmeier (standing), a detective with the Allen County Sheriff's Department in Fort Wayne, Indiana, listens to a caller's tip about the April Tinsley case on the set of *America's Most Wanted*.

HITTING THE AIRWAVES

Help Solve Cold Case, Part 2

Moments after *America's Most Wanted* aired a story Saturday evening about the 1988 rape and murder of 8-year-old April Tinsley—how her killer had left notes on young girls' bicycles years after the crime but had still managed to avoid capture—phones in the Washington studio started ringing.

Under the glare of multi-colored studio lights, about 20 hotline operators wearing headsets began taking tips on the case, and our special agent working to find the killer—along with detectives from Fort Wayne, Indiana, where the murder occurred—was standing by to talk with callers who might have critical information.

Although there would be no break in the Tinsley case on this night, nearly 50 tips were called in (most of them from the Fort Wayne area) providing information relating to the killer's distinctive notes, a paisley bedspread that appeared in a picture taken by the killer, and even the names of potential suspects.

"We are very pleased to get national publicity about this cold case," said Special Agent Robert E. King, with our Crimes Against Children Unit. King is one of the agents coordinating the Bureau's effort to help local law enforcement catch April Tinsley's killer. "Cases are solved through strong partnerships," he said, "and we are happy to be working with *America's Most Wanted*."

Our partnership with the popular TV show, known to many simply as "AMW," goes back a long way. In addition to having featured some of our unsolved fugitive cases since the show debuted in 1988, a member of our Violent Crimes Task Force in our Washington office has staffed the Saturday night show every week since 2007 to offer FBI assistance.

"We help out in any way we can," explained our agent during last week's program. "If tips or leads come in and we need to react in hours instead of days, we can contact our field offices immediately to aid local investigators."

AMW gets results. To date, the show has helped catch more than 1,000 fugitives worldwide, including a dozen criminals from our Ten Most Wanted Fugitives list. The premise is simple: Each week several stories are aired about missing persons or bad guys on the run. Viewers with information are encouraged to call in, and callers can remain anonymous unless they choose to leave their contact information.

Many of the hotline operators are working in or retired from law enforcement careers. Antonio Jones, an intelligence analyst in our Criminal Investigative Division at FBI Headquarters in Washington, has been an AMW hotline operator longer than anyone else—he started a few months after the show began 21 years ago.

During that time, Jones has fielded many calls that led to direct captures of fugitives. "When that hot call comes in," he said, "you know it right away. You get a cringe in your stomach."

Although there were no "hot" calls for the Tinsley case, Agent King said callers provided plenty of valuable tips to follow up on. "We want to help local authorities catch this guy, and we'll take every lead we can get."

We need your help. If you have any information about the April Tinsley case, contact your local FBI office or the Fort Wayne Police Department.

Antonio Jones (center), an FBI intelligence analyst, on the set of *America's Most Wanted*. He has been a hotline operator for 21 years, nearly as long as the show has been on the air.

WORK-AT-HOME SCAMS

Job One: Don't Take the Bait

Everyone's seen them—seductive work-at-home opportunities hyped in flyers tacked to telephone poles, in newspaper classifieds, in your e-mail, and all over the web, promising you hundreds or thousands of dollars a week for typing, stuffing envelopes, processing medical billing, etc. And it's just a phone call or mouse click away…

Might be tempting during these uncertain economic times, but beware of any offers that promise easy money for minimum effort—many are scams that fill the coffers of criminals.

Here are a few of the common work-at-home scams.

… **Advance-fee:** Starting a home-based business is easy! Just invest a few hundred dollars in inventory, set-up, and training materials, they say. Of course, if and when the materials do come, they are totally worthless…and you're stuck with the bill.

… **Counterfeit check-facilitated "mystery shopper:"** You're sent a hefty check and asked to deposit it into your bank account, then withdraw funds to shop and check out the service of local stores and wire transfer companies. You keep a small amount of the money for your "work," but then, as instructed, mail or wire the rest to your "employer." Sound good? One problem: the initial check was phony, and by the time your bank notifies you, your money is long gone and you're on the hook for the fake check.

… **Pyramid schemes:** You're hired as a "distributor" and shell out big bucks for promotional materials and product inventories with little value (like get-rich quick pamphlets). You're promised money for recruiting more distributors, so you talk friends and family into participating. The scheme grows exponentially but then falls apart—the only ones who make a profit are the criminals who started it.

… **Unknowing involvement in criminal activity:** Criminals—often located overseas—sometimes use unwitting victims to advance their operations, steal and launder money, and maintain anonymity. For example, they may "hire" you as a U.S.-based agent to receive and re-ship checks, merchandise, and solicitations to other victims…without you realizing it's all a ruse that leaves no trail back to the crooks.

Add identity theft to the mix. As if these schemes aren't bad enough, many also lead to identity theft. During the application process, you're often asked to provide personal information that can be used to steal from your bank account or establish new credit cards in your name.

On the job. A host of law enforcement and regulatory agencies, including the FBI, investigate these schemes and track down those responsible. But the most effective weapon against these fraudsters is you not falling for the scams in the first place.

A few tips:

- Contact the Better Business Bureau to determine the legitimacy of the company.
- Be suspicious when money is required up front for instructions or products.
- Don't provide personal information when first interacting with your prospective employer.
- Do your own research into legitimate work-at-home opportunities, using the "Work-at-Home Sourcebook" and other resources that may be available at your local library.
- Ask lots of questions of potential employers—legitimate companies will have answers for you!

And if you think you've been the victim of a work-at-home scam, file a complaint with the Federal Trade Commission's Consumer Sentinel or our Internet Crime Complaint Center.

Left: Daniel San Diego is wanted for his alleged role in the bombings of two San Francisco biotech facilities in 2003.

NEW MOST WANTED TERRORIST

First Domestic Fugitive Added to List

An animal rights extremist wanted for allegedly bombing two San Francisco-area office buildings in 2003 has been added to our Most Wanted Terrorists list—the first domestic terrorist to be included with international terrorists such as Usama Bin Laden.

Daniel Andreas San Diego, 31, should be considered armed and dangerous. His domestic acts of terror were planned to destroy property, to cause economic hardship for the companies he targeted, and possibly to take lives—one of his bombs was laced with nails to create potentially deadly shrapnel. We are offering a reward of up to $250,000 for information directly leading to his arrest.

"We have added San Diego to the Most Wanted Terrorists list to increase public awareness about this domestic terrorist fugitive and to aid in his arrest," said Michael J. Heimbach, Assistant Director of our Counterterrorism Division, at a press conference today at FBI Headquarters in Washington. "We will not relent until San Diego is apprehended and his potential for future acts of violence and destruction is eliminated."

Animal rights and environmental extremism pose a significant domestic terror threat. To date, extremists have been responsible for more than 1,800 criminal acts and more than $110 million in damages. Currently, we are investigating approximately 170 such extremist incidents across the country.

San Diego, known to be involved with a group called SHAC—Stop Huntingdon Animal Cruelty—is wanted for his alleged involvement in bombing two biotech facilities that did business with Huntingdon Life Sciences, a company that conducts animal experimentation for the medical and pharmaceutical industries.

The first bombing occurred on August 28, 2003, outside Chiron Life Science Center in Emeryville, California. When authorities responded, a second bomb was discovered, but exploded before it could be disarmed, raising the possibility that the device was planted specifically to target first responders.

Less than a month later, another bomb exploded outside a company based in Pleasanton, California. That bomb was made with metal nails to create more powerful shrapnel and destruction.

After each crime, claims of responsibility were posted on the Internet demanding that the businesses end their affiliation with Huntingdon Life Sciences. Future violence was threatened if these demands were not met. Fortunately, no one died in the explosions, but property damage was extensive.

San Diego was initially identified as a suspect after being stopped by a local police officer for a minor traffic violation in Pleasanton about an hour before the Pleasanton bombing. A subsequent search of his home and vehicle revealed bomb-making materials similar to those used in both attacks, and he was later indicted for the crimes.

San Diego has been on the run since October 2003. He is six feet tall, weighs about 160 pounds, and has brown hair and brown eyes. He wears glasses, is known to carry a 9mm handgun, has traveled internationally, and may be living out of the country, possibly in Costa Rica. He is a vegan and avoids consuming or wearing anything made with animal products. He also has distinctive tattoos—one on his chest is round and shows burning hills and plains with the words "It only takes a spark."

We need your help. If you have information you believe may be helpful to the investigation, contact our San Francisco office or submit a tip on our Tips and Public Leads page.

MORTGAGE FRAUD SCAM

'Dream Homes' Turns into Nightmare

The company had all the trappings of success—its top officials lived lavish lifestyles, kept a fleet of chauffeur-driven cars, and donated generously to charities. And it used slick marketing to sell its "Dream Homes Program," which promised to pay homeowners' mortgages in return for an up-front fee that would be invested in profitable business ventures.

But the dream turned into a $70 million nightmare for more than a thousand investors—among the latest victims of mortgage fraud.

According to federal grand jury indictments unsealed today, the five people behind Metro Dream Homes and the bogus mortgage payment program were actually running an elaborate deception—one eventually unraveled through the cooperative efforts of federal and state law enforcement agencies.

"The effects of this wide-ranging mortgage fraud scheme are particularly disturbing against the backdrop of today's economic environment," said Thomas J. Harrington, Executive Assistant Director of our Criminal, Cyber, Response, and Services Branch.

Here's how the scam worked:

- Between 2005 and 2007, victims were persuaded into investing at least $50,000 with Metro Dream Homes, either by refinancing their existing homes or buying new homes at inflated prices.
- Investors were told not to worry about high mortgages because Metro Dream Homes would pay their future monthly payments and pay off their mortgages within five to seven years using returns on the homeowner's original investment. Then the homeowner and Metro Dream Homes would own an equal interest in the home.
- Victims were told that their $50,000—not including an administrative fee of up to $5,000—would be used to fund investments in automated teller machines, flat-screen TV displays that carried commercial advertisements, and Touch-N-Buy electronic kiosks that sold telephone calling cards and other items.

FBI Executive Assistant Director Thomas J. Harrington of our Criminal, Cyber, Response, and Services Branch (right) and Assistant Attorney General Lanny A. Breuer of the Department of Justice's Criminal Division.

- To make the scam seem more legitimate, the company marketed its program through live presentations at posh hotels in Washington, D.C.; Baltimore; and even Beverly Hills, California.

In the end, it was a classic Ponzi scheme: the proceeds from later investors went to pay the mortgages of earlier investors. The ATMs, flat-screen TVs, and electronic kiosks never generated any meaningful revenue, federal prosecutors contend.

And the bulk of the money? It lined the defendants' pockets—with $200,000-a-year salaries, luxury cars, and travel to major sporting events like the 2007 Super Bowl.

By the time law enforcement shut down the company, homeowners had already invested about $70 million. When Metro Dream Homes stopped making the mortgage payments, the homeowners were left holding the bag. The defendants, meanwhile, are facing long prison terms for multiple counts of fraud, conspiracy to commit money laundering, and other charges.

At a press conference today at the Department of Justice to announce the indictments, Harrington said that to combat the recent "exponential rise in mortgage fraud investigations," the FBI has increased the number of agents who investigate mortgage fraud from 120 in 2007 to more 250 today. We participate in 18 mortgage fraud task forces and 47 working groups across the country.

If you have been the victim of a mortgage fraud scheme or have information about one, call your local FBI office or submit a tip electronically.

PRESIDENT RECOGNIZES FBI
In Visit to FBI Headquarters

On April 28, President Barack Obama paid a visit to FBI Headquarters in Washington, D.C., where he spoke privately with Bureau executives and addressed employees in the courtyard. Here are some pictures from the event.

With Director Mueller leading the way, President Obama enters the FBI courtyard to a cheering crowd.

President Obama tries on his new FBI Hat.

The President shows the crowd two teddy bears given to him by Director Mueller for his daughters, Sasha and Malia.

Before speaking to Bureau employees, President Obama met with Director Mueller and other executives.

The President smiles during his introduction by Director Mueller.

The President talks about how much the FBI has changed over the past century. "Part of what makes the FBI so unique is its ability to adapt to an evolving world," he said.

Hundreds of Bureau employees gathered to hear the President's speech and greet him afterward.

"With the attacks of 9/11, your mission became focused more than ever before on prevention—so that we have the capacity to uncover terrorist plots before they take hold," the President said.

Two Bureau employees share a laugh with the President.

The President thanks the men and women of the FBI for helping to keep the nation safe.

President Obama talks with FBI executives after his speech.

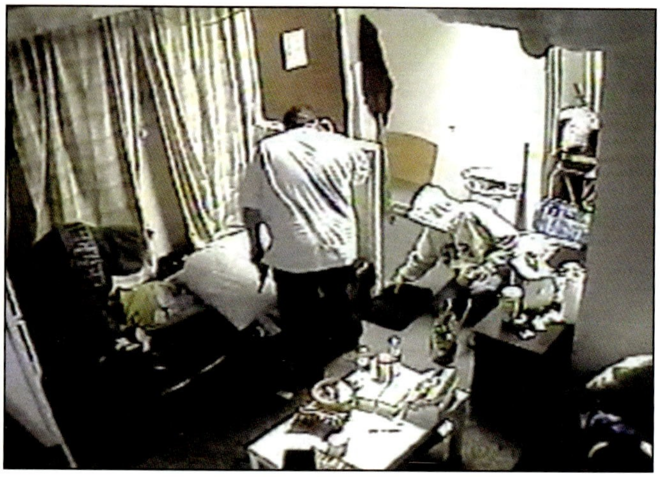

Left: Our MS-13 Task Force was able to resolve the case quickly because the victim came forward with security surveillance tapes of the robbery.

A COURAGEOUS VICTIM

Taking a Stand Against MS-13

After MS-13 gang members robbed a Houston beauty salon at gunpoint last January and sexually assaulted a salon employee, one of the gang members went a step further: he took the owner's picture so he knew exactly who she was. If she thought about going to the police, he said, she would be sorry. The owner was also told that from now on, she would be expected to pay $100 a week to the gang for "protection."

"What happened to this woman—robbery and extortion at the hands of MS-13—is not unusual," explained the agent in charge of our Houston Gang and Violent Crime Squad. "But her response—to stand up to the gang—was very unusual."

Though she feared for her life, the salon owner called the local police instead of paying the extortion money and was put in touch with our MS-13 task force. She had made a smart—and brave—decision.

MS-13, whose formal name is Mara Salvatrucha, is one of the largest Hispanic street gangs in the nation. According to the 2009 National Gang Threat Assessment, there could be as many as 50,000 MS-13 members worldwide, with 10,000 in America. The gang is known for its highly violent ways, and members are involved in all kinds of illegal activities, including drugs, robbery, extortion, weapons trafficking, and murder.

Larger gangs exist in Houston, our agent there said, but MS-13 is of particular concern because members are often heavily armed and well trained in the use of weapons and assault tactics.

Victims are usually so scared of MS-13 that they would rather pay extortion money than risk retribution. In Latin America, where MS-13 originated, such extortion schemes are common.

That is why the Houston salon owner's story is so remarkable. Despite her fear, she was also angry that the same crimes she saw in her native El Salvador were happening in the United States. So she came to us with security surveillance tapes in hand that showed the robbery and the faces of several gang members who had participated.

In a recently televised segment on MS-13 produced by the Spanish-language network Univision, the salon owner recounted her ordeal. "They threatened to kill me," she said of the gang members. "And I am very afraid for my life and my family." But she came forward, she said, because "I like to work and fight for what I want."

About a week after the robbery, with the owner refusing to pay protection money, two gang members drove by the salon and sprayed 17 bullets into the front door, shattering the windows of cars parked along the street in the process.

But thanks to the surveillance tape of the robbery and the salon owner's cooperation, it didn't take long to round up the gang members. In all, seven people were arrested, and six handguns and one shotgun were seized. The gang members face state charges of aggravated robbery—which can carry long prison sentences in Texas—and the possibilities of federal charges as well.

"This case is proof that victims of crime should not suffer in silence," our agent said. The salon owner, currently under the protection of the FBI, "was courageous to stand up to gang members, and as a result those gang members are now in jail."

And because of this case, other MS-13 extortion victims in Houston have come forward, our agent said. "If victims contact us, we can help."

THE RSA CONFERENCE
An After Action Report

Thousands of cyber security pros were there—from every industry and from across the world—networking... sharing the latest technologies and best practices...and soaking up expertise on such infinitely complex issues as botnets, cryptography, cyber warfare, hacking, cloud computing, data privacy, and insider and critical infrastructure threats.

It was the latest annual RSA Conference, held in San Francisco in late April—traditionally the largest gathering of computer security professionals anywhere.

We in the FBI were there in force as well, not just to absorb the latest and greatest on all things cyber but also to build upon our already deep partnerships with our colleagues in private industry and government (both foreign and domestic).

Our chief cyber exec Shawn Henry, who spoke at the conference, made news commenting on the Conficker worm. But he also had a lot to say about the seriousness of the overall cyber threat (his chief worries: terrorists, spies, and organized crime groups penetrating our defenses and wreaking havoc in cyberspace) and our commitment to taking the lead—along with the Department of Justice—in investigating and prosecuting cyber attacks.

The FBI's role is two-fold, he said: gathering, making sense of, and freely sharing intelligence on the universe of cyber threats and emerging trends (boosted by our understanding of all the major national security issues)...and rolling out targeted operations (often undercover) that take down these threats.

For us, the question of the conference—and beyond—is how far we are all willing to go collectively to protect our burgeoning computer networks. For all the power and possibilities it brings into our lives, the Internet and everything connected to it opens the door to our most sensitive financial, defense, commercial, and personal information. By putting our most important systems and data online, we couldn't have created a better feeding ground for terrorists, spies, and criminals of all kinds.

It boils down to this: we are building our lives around our cyber networks. Are we ready to work together to defend them?

FBI Assistant Director Shawn Henry speaks at the recent RSA cyber security conference in San Francisco.

The FBI certainly is. For our part, we're committed to:

- Continuing to work through such channels as InfraGard to exchange threat information;
- Sharing intelligence on a targeted basis in response to a specific threat to a particular sector (i.e., banks), even if it might impact our investigations ("We'll get the bad guy later," says Henry);
- Reaching out to more CEOs and business execs to make sure they fully understand the threat and that they allocate resources and enact policies that help provide their networks with day-to-day protection;
- Building relationships with our counterparts overseas, where most of our investigations start or end; and
- Working with the Department of Homeland Security and other agencies to defend critical infrastructure.

At the same time, we need lots of support and advice from businesses, academia, and government:

- Most importantly, we need intelligence from cyber experts like those at the conference—details on possible suspects and victims and the tools, tactics, and procedures used in attacks.
- We need companies to report incidents, even when it's not convenient to do so. Henry said, "I know trust is an important aspect of this sharing, and I hope you continue to trust that I will maintain your confidentiality, use the information you give me wisely, and actually have an impact on the threat."

As was echoed throughout the conference, trust and cooperation are our best weapons for protecting cyberspace—today and in the future.

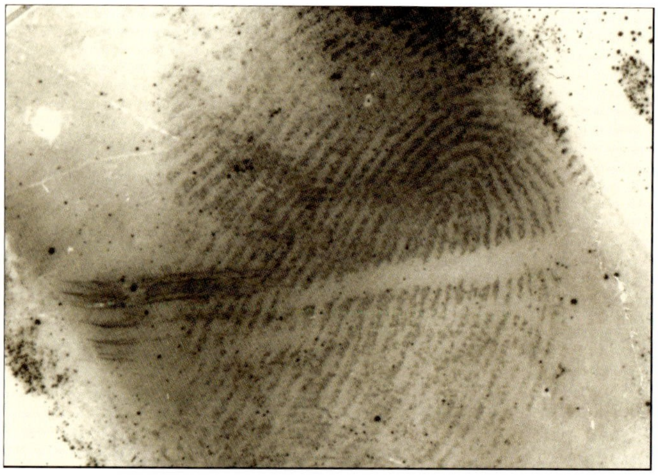

Left: Partial latent fingerprint

30-YEAR-OLD MURDER SOLVED

By the 'Hit of the Year'

May 1977. A man is beaten to death in a suburb of San Diego. Police find a smudged latent print at the scene and search it against California state fingerprint files. No match is found, no leads developed, no suspect identified.

May 2007. The investigating agency—the Escondido Police Department—creates a cold case squad and reopens the 1977 murder case. This time around, law enforcement is able to take advantage of an investigative tool that was not in existence 30 years earlier—the FBI's Integrated Automated Fingerprint Identification System (IAFIS) that ties together fingerprint records from around the country. Several hits are made in IAFIS and a suspect is identified.

This is just one example of the thousands of cases investigated every year by state and local law enforcement around the country that get an assist from IAFIS. It was also the case chosen by our Criminal Justice Information Services (CJIS) Division to receive its 2008 IAFIS "Hit of the Year" award presented last year.

The Hit of the Year is the brainchild of our CJIS Division, which created the award in 2007 in response to a survey of law enforcement agencies that were asking for more details of major cases solved when IAFIS identified latent prints. The award, presented annually at the International Association for Identification conference, was given out for the first time in 2007. Details about the award-winning case are also published in a CJIS publication available online to all law enforcement.

The Escondido case was selected for recognition because of the persistence of the cold case squad members and the California state fingerprint analyst. Their efforts led to not only an identification but an arrest as well…30 years after the murder.

Here are some of the case details.

Shortly after the Escondido Police Department cold case squad was formed, the team began looking into the 1977 murder. In addition to two homicide detectives, members of the team included two retired officers—one who had actually been on patrol in Escondido the night of the murder—and a retired FBI agent.

The squad interviewed more than 30 people across the country and reviewed crime scene photos. They also submitted photographs of the smudged print to the California Department of Justice, where a latent print analyst checked state databases as well as the Bureau's IAFIS.

Within 16 minutes, IAFIS kicked out 20 possible matches for comparison. The state analyst determined a definite match—to a convicted murderer who had been arrested in several states and was currently living in Reno, Nevada, out on lifetime parole after the murder of a Reno woman.

The suspect was arrested by Reno authorities and extradited to San Diego. He pled guilty to the murder of the Escondido man and is now back in prison, where he belongs.

Looking for nominations.

If you work at a police department and you think you've got a great case for consideration for the 2009 Hit of the Year, e-mail the details to the CJIS Division's Latent Technology Development Team at ltdt@leo.gov. The award will be presented in August at the International Association for Identification conference in Tampa. Best of luck!

NATIONAL POLICE WEEK 2009

Honoring Those Who Serve

The FBI joined the nation in observing National Police Week from May 10-16, 2009. The following are photos from a few of the events.

Unity Tour representatives make an etching of the name of a fallen comrade from the wall at the National Law Enforcement Officers Memorial.

Approximately 1,200 law enforcement officers took part in the Police Unity Tour this year as a way to pay tribute to their fellow officers killed in the line of duty.

The bicyclists, some who began their ride hundreds of miles away, are greeted enthusiastically by family, friends, and other supporters as they arrive at the National Law Enforcement Officers Memorial.

Along with Jennifer Thacker, national president of Concerns of Police Survivors (COPS), U.S. Attorney General Eric Holder (right) and FBI Director Robert Mueller (left) recite the Pledge of Allegiance during the 21st annual Candlelight Vigil for slain officers held May 13, 2009, at the National Law Enforcement Officers Memorial.

FBI Director Robert Mueller, COPS president Jennifer Thacker, and Attorney General Eric Holder, among others, holding candles in memory of the fallen officers.

May 15, 2009

Left: The FBI Facebook page contains videos and timely news updates.

THE FBI ON FACEBOOK

And YouTube. And Twitter. And More.

Over the past few years we've rolled out a number of new web initiatives—including an e-mail alert service, syndicated news feeds, and a series of podcasts and widgets—that make it easier for you to help us track down wanted fugitives and missing kids, to submit tips on terrorism and crime, and to get our latest news and information.

Today, we're announcing the launch of our latest suite of tools. We've recently set up shop in several social media websites, including:

- **Facebook**, where you can follow our news, check out our photos and videos, and become a "fan";
- **YouTube**, where you can watch our videos and connect back to our main website for job postings and other content; and
- **Twitter**, where you can receive our tweets on breaking news and other useful information.

To reach out to the public, we need to be where people are—and we know tens of millions of people spend their time in social media sites," says John Miller, head of FBI Public Affairs. "Adding our fugitives, missing kids, threat and scam warnings, and other information into these sites is an extension of what we've done for decades—enlisting the help and support of concerned citizens around the globe to keep communities safer."

We are moving forward on other social media fronts as well.

... **More widgets.** Our widgets have been enormously popular, and we plan to build more in the coming weeks. "Our first four widgets alone have brought more than 2.5 million people to our website," points out Jonathan Cox, a management analyst in the Office of Public Affairs who spearheaded their development. "And our latest Most Wanted widget averages more than a thousand views a day." The new high-end widget was built using Flash, XML, and ActionScript and can be shared virally through social media websites such as Facebook, MySpace, and Blogger, says Michael Litchfield, the web developer who built it for the FBI. "I was excited to work on it and thought it was a great way to market the Bureau to a new generation."

... **Fugitives at your fingertips.** A company called NIC—founded by an ex-law enforcement officer—has built a free "Most Wanted" iPhone and iPod Touch application based on our newest widget and fueled by our RSS feeds. More than 350,000 people in 80 countries worldwide have already downloaded the app since it debuted in February. "Now, NIC is building a second-generation version that will use geo-location information to enable you to easily submit tips to your local FBI office," says Harry Herington, Chairman of the Board and CEO of NIC. It will include FBI Twitter feeds and connections to our Facebook and YouTube sites. NIC is also developing an iPhone application focused specifically on missing kids that will include Amber Alerts, pictures, and potentially live data to help law enforcement and the families of missing children.

... **Virtual billboards and kiosks.** We're doing pilot tests in Second Life—a free 3-D world inhabited by millions of people worldwide—for virtual billboards and kiosks that show the mugs of our Ten Most Wanted fugitives and connect people to FBI jobs, our Internet Crime Complaint Center, and the wanted posters of cyber criminals.

Jonathan Cox—along with graphic artist Scott Carmine—designed our first virtual billboards for sites like Second Life and sees them as the wave of the future. "Unlike 10 years ago, almost everyone today has had an experience connecting online through virtual media, whether through a gaming console or popular sites like Second Life," Cox said. "The ease at which information can be transferred, ideas can be exposed, and technology can be shared in virtual worlds will hopefully lead to the arrest of a fugitive or the location of a missing child in the near future."

IN SEARCH OF A KILLER

Help Solve Cold Case, Part 3

On a beautiful spring morning in the farm country outside Fort Wayne, Indiana, one of our agents knocks on the front door of a well-kept home. In this quiet neighborhood nearly 20 years ago, an incredible clue appeared in a murder case—a message scrawled on a barn door by the murderer himself.

"I killed 8-year-old April Marie Tinsley," it said. And there was also this: "I will kill again."

A woman answers the door—she had been working in her garden—and our agent—part of a special FBI team working with Indiana law enforcement to help solve the 1988 abduction and murder—introduces himself, shows his badge, and asks for her help. Did she live here when the barn door message was discovered in 1990? Was there anyone in the neighborhood at the time who made her feel uncomfortable? Did she know anyone who still used a Polaroid camera?

This scene was being repeated in many Fort Wayne neighborhoods, as the cold case we have written about recently is getting a fresh look by Indiana law enforcement and our Child Abduction Rapid Deployment (CARD) Team.

Working with the National Center for Missing & Exploited Children, the Fort Wayne Police Department, the Allen County Sheriff's Department, and the Indiana State Police, the CARD Team set up a command post in Fort Wayne earlier this month to manage about 75 agents, detectives, analysts, and command staff involved in the investigation and to track the leads—old and new.

One reason the Tinsley case is getting such close scrutiny after all these years is public safety: as recently as 2004, the killer left provocative, threatening notes around Fort Wayne taking credit for the murder.

The CARD Team was created to bring together a variety of experts in child abduction cases who could help local authorities on the ground. So about a dozen team members from all over the country arrived in Fort Wayne and got to work on the Tinsley case:

- Agents with our Crimes Against Children Unit received packets—some with suspects' criminal histories and last known addresses—with leads to investigate.

An FBI crime analyst (left) provides support to agents in the field investigating the April Tinsley case.

- Members of our Behavioral Analysis Unit, who assess offenders' personalities and possible motives, crafted a list of interview questions and later issued a profile of the killer based on existing evidence.
- Coordinators from our National Center for the Analysis of Violent Crime and representatives from our Violent Criminal Apprehension Program were stationed at command post computer terminals, ready to supply investigators in the field with everything from license plate checks to satellite maps.

"Our approach with this case is that no lead is too small to work," said Special Agent Robert E. King, one of the agents leading the CARD Team investigation.

The entire effort was a cooperative one. Our agents paired with local detectives—25 two-person teams worked day and night shifts—to re-canvass neighborhoods, conduct interviews, and ask for DNA samples from possible suspects. Investigators then entered their findings into our new crisis management system.

So far, April Tinsley's killer remains at large, but there is always another lead to pursue and another door to knock on.

Left: A New York FBI employee is greeted at City Hall by New York FBI Assistant Director in Charge Joseph M. Demarest and, from right foreground, New York's Governor David A. Paterson, Police Commissioner Raymond W. Kelly, and Mayor Michael R. Bloomberg.

NEW YORK SAYS THANKS

To Investigators of Foiled Bomb Plot

In light of the May 20 arrest of four people charged with plotting to blow up Jewish targets and shoot down military planes in New York, about 70 investigators from local, state, and federal agencies who worked the terrorism case were honored today in a ceremony at New York City Hall.

New York City Mayor Michael Bloomberg—along with New York Governor David Paterson, New York City Police Commissioner Raymond Kelly, and New York FBI Assistant Director in Charge (ADIC) Joseph Demarest—presented each member of the group with a certificate of appreciation for their work on the case.

Thanking the investigators, Mayor Bloomberg said, "We know we live in very dangerous times, but thankfully we have an excellent system of defenses to protect us. And in the first line of these defenses are our superb law enforcement officers, including those we honor today."

Demarest stressed the importance of continuing cooperation among all the members of the New York Joint Terrorism Task Force and the other law enforcement agencies who participated in the year-long investigation.

The four defendants in the case have been charged with conspiracy to use weapons of mass destruction in the United States and conspiracy to acquire and use anti-aircraft missiles.

The four allegedly plotted to detonate explosives near a synagogue in the Riverdale section of the Bronx, New York and to shoot military planes located at the New York Air National Guard Base at Stewart Airport in Newburgh, New York. They obtained what they thought were three Improvised Explosive Devices (IEDs) and a Stinger surface-to-air guided missile from a source. Their "source" turned out to be an FBI informant who gave them a Stinger that wasn't capable of being fired and IEDs that contained over 30 pounds of inert C-4 plastic explosives.

The mayor said that the case was the result of the cooperative efforts of several agencies, including the U.S. Attorney's Office for the Southern District of New York, the FBI, the New York Police Department, the Newburgh City Police Department, the Town of New Windsor Police Department, the U.S. Air Force Office of Special Investigations, and the New York State Office of Homeland Security.

LOOKING FOR OUR CHILDREN

'National Missing Children's Day 2009'

These are just a very few of the children who are far away from home tonight.

Please take a minute to look at all the faces on our Kidnapping and Missing Persons webpage and see if you can identify Crystal, Chioma, Steven, or any of the other children listed there with their stories.

Please also take a look at the faces of the children who have been kidnapped by a parent—Camille and the other 39 kids.

And we hope you'll visit our Crimes Against Children webpage to learn all you can about what a dangerous world it can be for our kids…and our Resources for Parents webpage to learn how to protect them in today's world.

Last: join us in honoring the law enforcement officers and others recognized as part of National Missing Children's day, including FBI Agents Alexis Carpinteri, Michael D. Leverock, and Greg Ryman.

Note: The children pictured or identified here may have been located since the above information was posted on our website. Please check our Wanted by the FBI website or contact your local FBI office for up-to-date information.

May 27, 2009

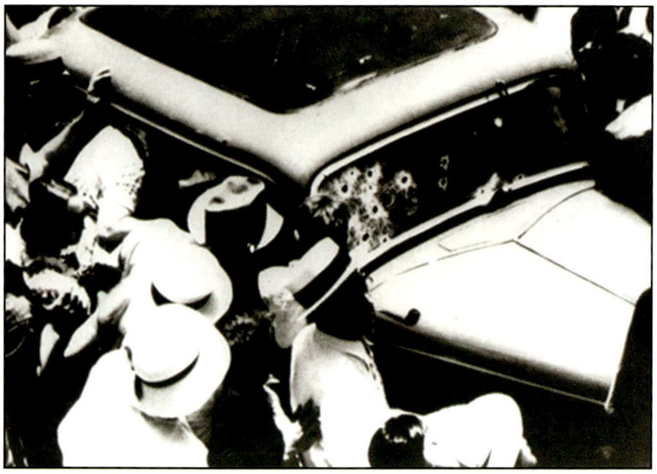

Left: A crowd gathers around Bonnie and Clyde's bullet-ridden sedan not long after the fatal ambush.

BONNIE AND CLYDE REDUX

The Year of the Gangster, Part 3

It was 75 years ago this past Saturday—on the morning of May 23, 1934—that Clyde Barrow and Bonnie Parker drove their Ford sedan down a dusty back road in Louisiana and straight into an ambush.

A posse of heavily-armed lawmen put an end to the infamous crime couple's deadly reign—but it was really just the beginning of the nation's fascination with the star-crossed lovers, whose story is still being told today.

Now, there's a little bit more to talk about.

For the first time, we're releasing on our website nearly 1,000 pages of new material on our investigations of Bonnie and Clyde and their partners in crime—including some pictures that you see here. The information represents the investigative case records of our Dallas Field Office, which were uncovered in the course of preparing a historical exhibit in Dallas and disclosed last year.

These pages describe the Bureau's involvement in the pursuit of Bonnie and Clyde, which began almost exactly a year before their deaths when we discovered evidence that they had crossed state lines in a stolen car. By the time we joined the hunt, the pair had been crisscrossing the Midwest, chased by every level of law enforcement across eight states—stealing cars, robbing banks and gas stations, taking hostages, and even gunning down police officers and innocent bystanders alike. Their rapid-fire movements and connections were such that our agents in Dallas, New Orleans, Detroit, Kansas City, Oklahoma City, San Antonio, St. Louis, and elsewhere were soon involved.

Our Dallas file clearly shows how the many different levels of law enforcement worked together closely in the hunt for Bonnie and Clyde. They shared information, leads, and informants, with the FBI often acting as a clearinghouse for the spread of information across the Midwest.

New Orleans Division Special Agent Lester Kindell, for example, played a central role in this cooperative effort to track the fugitives in Louisiana and parts of Texas, joining hands with former Texas Ranger Frank Hamer and others. Kindell was also closely involved in discussions that led to the final confrontation with Bonnie and Clyde, although he did not participate in the fatal ambush.

Clyde Barrow poses by a road sign

The four parts of this file add to the information we've already made available on these notorious criminals, and we hope that they lead to new understandings of law enforcement and crime during what we are calling "The Year of the Gangster."

Editor's note: The Year of the Gangster, Part 2 was a video feature story on the shoot-out with John Dillinger and 'Baby Face' Nelson in the woods of Wisconsin. To view the video go to http://www.fbi.gov/multimedia/bohemia042309/bohemia042309.htm.

CRIME IS DOWN
According to Our Preliminary Stats

For the second year in row, the number of violent crimes declined across the country—a total of 2.5 percent during 2008 compared to the previous year—according to our just-released *Preliminary Annual Uniform Crime Report*.

And more good news: the number of property crimes decreased nationally as well—1.6 percent—over 2007 levels. In fact, property crime has fallen every year since 2003.

Some highlights from this report:

- All four of the violent crime offense categories declined nationwide: murder and nonnegligent manslaughter (down 4.4 percent), aggravated assault (down 3.2 percent), forcible rape (down 2.2 percent), and robbery (down 1.1 percent).
- While violent crimes like murder, forcible rape, and robberies in cities with one million or more residents decreased, cities with less than 10,000 residents reported increases in those same categories (murder up 5.5 percent, forcible rape up 1.4 percent, robbery up 3.9 percent).
- Nationwide, burglaries were the only property crime to show an increase (up 1.3 percent), while thefts decreased (down 0.6 percent) as did motor vehicle thefts (down a whopping 13.1 percent!).
- Arson offenses, tracked separately from other property crimes, declined in all four regions of the country—Northeast, South, Midwest, and West. The largest decrease was in the West (down 5.9 percent).

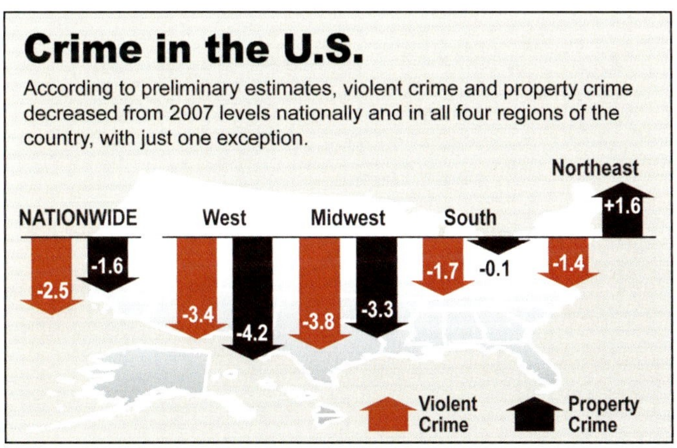

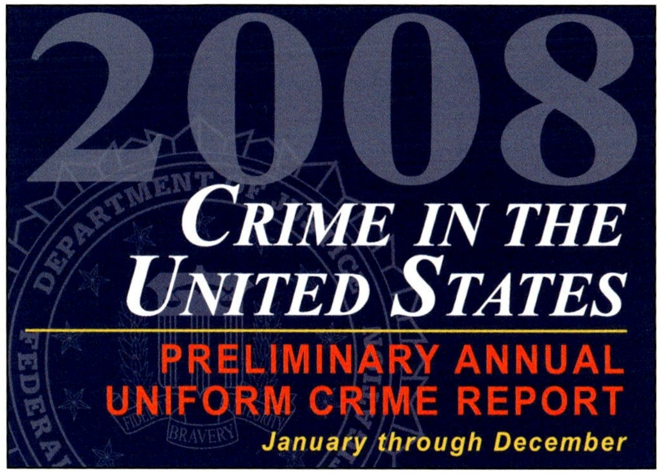

The reason for the preliminary report? To get—as quickly as possible—some of the basic data we collected on crime in 2008 into the hands of law enforcement, community leaders, criminologists, and others in a position to begin analyzing the problems, allocating resources, and implementing prevention strategies.

Cooperative efforts. This preliminary report was based on data sent to us by our partners from 12,750 city, county, college and university, state, tribal, and federal agencies around the nation.

Two things to remember about our crime stats:

- First, many entities—news media, tourism agencies, and other groups with an interest in crime—use figures from our crime reports to compile rankings of cities and counties. Such rankings are misleading, as there are many variables that impact the nature and the extent of crime in different geographic locations.
- The FBI doesn't interpret the data; we leave the number-crunching and in-depth analysis to criminologists, state and local law enforcement agencies, and other experts. We do, however, work closely with our partners to develop strategies to combat and prevent violence and crime in our communities.

Check back with us in the fall for the complete 2008 *Crime in the United States report*.

BACK TO BASICS

The Director on the Financial Crisis

When our New York agents busted 13 people last week for mortgage scams involving properties worth more than $10 million, many of those arrested claimed they were just making money the same way as everyone else.

Really?

"The individuals involved in the scams consistently stated that everyone in the mortgage industry was doing this, so they assumed it was the norm and therefore legal," said one of our case agents.

And what were they allegedly doing? Lying to homeowners—tricking them into selling their homes to help erase their debts, but in the end often causing them to get evicted. Deliberately putting false information on loan applications so they could flip properties for a profit. Promising straw buyers the moon (We'll make your mortgage payments for months!) only to renege and cause the buyers to default on their loans. And on and on, all while pocketing big bucks.

Has it gotten that bad—that people believe such deceptions and crimes are just the normal way of doing business?

Apparently so, and on Tuesday, Director Robert Mueller was in New York—the financial capital of the world—to talk about this very issue: the lack of integrity in the marketplace, the boardroom, and the halls of government…and the FBI's role in combating it, including using our intelligence gathering capabilities to help prevent new financial threats.

"This is by no means the first financial crisis we have had, nor is it the first instance of bad business judgment or unadulterated greed," Mueller said at the Economic Club of New York. But many of today's financial crimes, he noted, involve losses "that once would have been unthinkable."

From our perspective alone, the numbers are sobering:

- We are currently investigating more than 2,400 mortgage fraud matters—more than double the number from two years ago. And we have doubled the number of agents working these cases.
- We have more than 580 corporate fraud and 1,300 securities fraud investigations open—some (like the Madoff case) representing billions in losses.
- In the area of public corruption, we have more than 2,500 pending cases. In the past two years, our investigations have helped convict nearly 1,700 officials who have violated the public trust.

Our approach throughout has been to use our full suite of investigative tools to identify key players and dismantle larger criminal rings…to pull together specialized expertise where we need it (such as our specially-trained Corporate Fraud Response Team that can respond at a moment's notice to complex cases nationwide)…and just as importantly, to use our intelligence capabilities to spot trends on the horizon.

One trend that the Director spoke of in detail involves what he called "the next wave of cases" for the FBI: fraud and corruption involving TARP funds and the stimulus package. He said that we are working with a variety of partners to identify where the money is going and for what purpose to head off potential problems.

Going forward, Mueller stressed the need for "independent board members, auditors, and outside counsel" to help keep organizations honest. "If this financial crisis has taught us anything," he said," it may be that it is time for a cultural shift—a 'back to basics' approach that incorporates sound business judgment, risk assessment, and integrity, from the top down."

Indeed.

ABUSE OF TRUST

The Case of the Crooked Border Official

She seemed to be serving the nation, but she was really working for a band of drug traffickers for a boatload of cash…

Americans trust that their public servants will use their positions of power lawfully—that's why crimes involving the breach of this trust is our top criminal investigative priority. And while we investigate all kinds of public corruption, perhaps the one that most directly threatens our nation's security and well-being involves our borders.

Keep in mind that each day, thousands of honest and dedicated men and women patrol our borders, screening travelers and goods for possible threats to our homeland. Yet their hard work is sometimes overshadowed by an occasional crooked official—like former customs inspector Margarita Crispin who, for her own financial gain, looked the other way while drug traffickers moved illegal drugs across the U.S.-Mexican border.

How it began

In late 2004, Immigration and Customs Enforcement (ICE) contacted our field office in El Paso, Texas. One of their informants reported that Crispin was allowing shipments of illegal drugs into the U.S. through her border post in El Paso.

Building the case

Together with our partner agencies—ICE, the Department of Homeland Security's Inspector General, Customs and Border Protection, and the Drug Enforcement Administration—we began surveilling Crispin. We learned that not long after she was hired, Crispin—who lived meagerly in El Paso—acquired two expensive homes in Mexico, along with several luxury vehicles, but she attempted to cover her tracks with straw buyers. We also discovered that she socialized with known drug traffickers.

In May 2006, a strange incident in Crispin's assigned vehicle lane at the border crossing aroused our suspicions even more: a van going through her lane ran out of gas, and its driver jumped out and ran back across the border to Mexico. When other inspectors opened the van doors, they found nearly 6,000 pounds of marijuana…in plain view. Crispin couldn't explain why that van was in her lane, and later that day she went home "sick."

When this van ran out of gas in Crispin's lane at the border crossing, its driver ran off and left behind 6,000 pounds of marijuana.

The turning point

For the next year, we continued to watch her. In July 2007, we received information that a truck loaded with marijuana would be crossing through Crispin's lane. On July 7, that vehicle appeared. It was stopped and seized after it passed her inspection and was found to be packed with about 1,500 pounds of marijuana. This seizure—along with intelligence information, analysis of Crispin's finances, telephone toll records, witness interviews, and documented surveillance—was enough for a federal indictment.

On July 25, 2007, Margarita Crispin reported for work, just like any other day. Only this time federal officers were there to greet her…and walked her out in handcuffs. In April 2008, she pled guilty and was sentenced to 240 months in prison for conspiring to import drugs, but beyond that, for abusing the public trust.

The end game

"The Crispin case," says El Paso Special Agent in Charge David Cuthbertson, "exemplifies our commitment to removing those few bad apples from the ranks of hard-working public servants everywhere…even one case like this is one too many."

Last year alone, the FBI worked nearly 2,500 public corruption cases and saw convictions of more than 700 dishonest public servants around the nation.

Left: One of hundreds of manuscripts—this one published in 1617—recovered from the home of John Sisto.

ARRIVEDERCI

Recovered Italian Artifacts Headed Home

In March 2007, members of the Berwyn, Illinois Police Department entered the home of a recently deceased man at the request of his son. What they found in that small house in a Chicago suburb eventually reverberated nearly 5,000 miles away: the late owner of the home—John Sisto—had been haphazardly storing more than 3,500 suspected antiquities from Italy in boxes, in piles on the floor, and on bookshelves.

On Monday, some of those items were on public display for the first time in years during a press conference with our partners—when Special Agent in Charge Robert Grant of our Chicago office announced that approximately 1,600 of them would be returned to Italian authorities.

Bountiful discovery. When Berwyn police discovered the treasure trove of what appeared to be historical items—like books, parchments, documents, and works of art—they contacted the Chicago FBI for assistance in identifying the items. That's when members of our Art Crime Team began an investigation, working closely with the Berwyn police, our Legal Attaché in Rome, the Italian Command for the Protection of Cultural Heritage, and the Italian Ministry for Cultural Assets and Activities.

After moving the artifacts to our Chicago office, investigators photographed and catalogued each item. Pictures were sent to subject matter experts in Italy, who identified the items as having come from the Bari region of Italy. These experts traveled to the U.S. twice for a close-up look at the rest of the inventory. After conferring with various churches, archives, libraries, and owners of private collections in Italy, they determined that about 1,600 of the items had been stolen and should be returned.

Included among the items were:

- 380 manuscripts and parchments, including a 1662 doctoral diploma and writings by kings, emperors, and popes;
- 1,000 books dating from the 17th and 18th centuries;
- A book preface written by Benito Mussolini; and
- Religious artifacts and relics, including a shoe worn by a clergyman and about 100 terra cotta heads given as offerings to the Roman Catholic Church.

A 4th century B.C. pottery jar from Southern Italy.

How did John Sisto amass such a collection? We think that in most instances the items were secretly shipped to Sisto from his father—an Italian citizen living in Italy—from the early 1960s until the older man's death in 1982. John Sisto was probably instructed by his father to sell the items at the antique shop he was running at the time, but he didn't have much luck. John Sisto also made an attempt to get various museums and libraries interested in his collection, but that didn't pan out either, so he simply stored most of the items in his home.

It appeared that Sisto, who spent a great deal of his time translating and studying the various manuscripts and parchments, was more interested in the historical significance of the items than their monetary value.

Because the principals in this case are deceased, no charges will be filed in the United States. Nonetheless, we are pleased that these priceless artifacts will be returning home to their historical birthplace, thanks to the joint efforts of the Berwyn Police Department, Italian authorities, our field office in Chicago, and the family of John Sisto. *Grazie e buona fortuna.*

PONZI SCHEME INDICTMENTS

Five Charged in $7 Billion Ploy

Today in Washington, D.C., the FBI, Department of Justice, and our partner agencies announced the unsealing of an indictment in the Southern District of Texas related to a multi-billion dollar Ponzi scheme that victimized thousands in the U.S. and abroad.

The indictment charges Robert Allen Stanford, the sole shareholder of the Houston-based Stanford Financial Group and other affiliated companies, with defrauding investors who purchased approximately $7 billion in certificates of deposit administered by Stanford International Bank, an offshore bank located on the island of Antigua.

Charges against Stanford, along with four other individuals, include conspiracy to commit mail fraud, mail fraud and securities fraud, wire fraud, obstructing an investigation by the Securities and Exchange Commission (SEC), and conspiracy to commit money laundering.

Said Lanny Breuer, Assistant Attorney General for the Department of Justice's Criminal Division, "As today's charges make clear, the Department will vigorously root out and expose financial crimes that wreak havoc on innocent investors."

Also charged were:

- **Laura Pendergest-Holt**, chief investment officer of Stanford Financial Group and a member of Stanford International Bank's investment committee, who had also been previously charged with obstruction of justice in a separate SEC proceeding;
- **Gilberto Lopez**, Stanford Financial Group's chief accounting officer;
- **Mark Kuhrt**, global controller for Stanford Financial Group; and
- **Leroy King**, administrator and chief executive officer of the Financial Services Regulatory Commission, the regulator for Antigua and Barbuda's financial services industry. King allegedly accepted bribes to ensure that Stanford International Bank was not subject to close scrutiny by Antiguan or U.S. regulators.

Additionally, a criminal information was unsealed charging James M. Davis, Stanford Financial Group's chief financial officer, for his role in the scheme, along with an indictment charging another former Stanford Financial Group employee with destroying company records.

Above: Kevin Perkins, assistant director of the FBI Criminal Investigative Division, comments on indictments handed down in the alleged $7 billion Ponzi scheme.

The scam. According to the indictment, Stanford International Bank offered—through its network of financial advisors—CDs with higher (and ultimately bogus) rates of return than those available through CDs offered by U.S. banks. Stanford and his co-conspirators also misrepresented to clients the actual financial condition of Stanford International Bank, its investment strategy, and the extent of its regulatory oversight by Antiguan authorities.

While collecting billions from his investors, who placed their trust and in some cases their life savings with him, Stanford and his co-defendants were allegedly misusing and misappropriating most of these assets, including diverting at least $1.6 billion into undisclosed personal loans to Stanford himself.

According to FBI Assistant Director Kevin Perkins, in the past 18 months, we've opened 100 new cases into these financial scams, many involving losses of more than $20 million. "Ponzi schemes and other securities fraud investigations are one of the top priorities of the FBI's Criminal Investigative Division," said Perkins. "We recognize the enormous impact these crimes have on the economy as a whole and on the trust of investors."

The case was worked jointly by the Department of Justice, FBI, Internal Revenue Service, U.S. Postal Inspection Service, and SEC.

Left: Emergency responders at the Metrorail crash on the border of Maryland and Washington, D.C.

CRASH SCENE ASSISTANCE

Lending a Hand to NTSB

When two Metro trains collided in Washington yesterday afternoon, killing at least nine and injuring more than 75 others, scores of first responders led by the District of Columbia Fire Department and the Washington Metropolitan Police Department, along with other law enforcement agencies—including the FBI—arrived on the scene.

Because the accident happened within the National Capital Region, our National Capital Response Squad and other Bureau personnel swung into action at the request of the National Transportation Safety Board (NTSB) to assist with evidence recovery and victim identification.

"We have been here since the beginning," said Special Agent Christopher Combs, who heads the National Capital Response Squad out of our Washington Field Office. Combs said about 20 Bureau personnel from his squad and others are working at the crash scene and will remain there as long as NTSB needs them.

In addition to Combs' squad, also on hand are members of our Washington, Pittsburgh, and Laboratory Division-based Evidence Response Teams (ERTs), other area personnel, and a variety of Bureau equipment, including a mobile command center. Also, soon after the crash—the worst in Metro's history—we ramped up our Command and Tactical Operations Center at the Washington Field Office to coordinate Bureau efforts at the scene.

Beyond being good neighbors, the Bureau has agreements with all our National Capital Region partners, the NTSB, and other federal agencies to provide support if requested in the event of a crisis like this one.

Below: FBI Evidence Response Team personnel at Metrorail train crash.

A MAJOR CRACKDOWN
On Health Care Fraud

This afternoon, we joined with the Department of Justice and the Department of Health and Human Services in announcing the unsealing of indictments against 53 people in a combined enforcement effort specifically targeting fraud schemes that threaten Medicare…and our country's most vulnerable citizens—seniors, people with disabilities, and low-income Americans.

Agents from the FBI and the Health and Human Services (HHS) Inspector General's Office have already begun arresting the defendants in Detroit and Miami. These defendants were the subjects of several separate health care fraud investigations by the new Detroit Medicare Fraud Strike Force, comprised of FBI and HHS agents and Department of Justice (DOJ) prosecutors. Combined, the subjects are accused of conspiring to submit more than $50 million in false claims to Medicare.

Today's arrests involved at least nine Medicare provider companies and a number of company executives, doctors, therapists, medical recruiters, medical assistants, and even some Medicare beneficiaries who were willing to go along with the schemes in exchange for money.

The two primary types of fraud schemes being perpetrated include:

- **Physical therapy/occupational therapy fraud:** The crux of these schemes was billing Medicare for services not rendered. In most cases, the subjects created fictitious patient files by paying Medicare beneficiaries, therapists, and doctors to fill out and sign documentation indicating services had been provided when in fact they had not been. These phony files were then systematically distributed to Medicare providers for illicit billing.
- **Infusion therapy fraud:** Several Michigan infusion therapy companies providing medication for AIDS, HIV-positive, and Hepatitis C patients were allegedly billing Medicare for services not actually performed, were medically unnecessary, or were medically unlikely (medicines not normally prescribed for particular conditions). Note: infusion therapy involves giving medicine intravenously to patients whose conditions are so severe they can't be treated with oral medication.

To investigate health care fraud, Director Robert Mueller said that the FBI is focused on "partnerships, intelligence, and information-sharing." He also explained how our sophisticated investigative techniques—from undercover operations to wiretaps—can be used to "not only collect evidence for prosecution, but to find and stop criminals before the schemes spread."

FBI Director Mueller comments on the indictments as HHS Secretary Kathleen Sebelius looks on.

Bringing the HEAT. Today's announcement came a month after Attorney General Eric Holder and HHS Secretary Kathleen Sebelius announced the creation of a task force—the Health Care Fraud Prevention and Enforcement Action Team, or HEAT—to continue ramping up coordinated efforts against health care fraud. HEAT is comprised of DOJ and HHS senior leaders who will work towards increasing cooperation, intelligence sharing, and training among their investigators, agents, and prosecutors. Medicare strike forces will figure prominently in HEAT's efforts.

The first such strike force was established in Miami in 2007, followed by a second in Los Angeles and two more recently in Detroit and Houston—all areas of the country with concentrated Medicare fraud activity. And just yesterday, indictments in a $100 million Medicare and Medicaid scheme were announced in Miami.

Health care fraud, according to Director Mueller, is "not a victimless crime—every person who struggles to pay for health care benefits; every older person who worries about Medicare's ability to cover them; every taxpayer who helps fund these programs—they are all victims." All good reasons why we take our responsibility to investigate health care fraud very seriously.

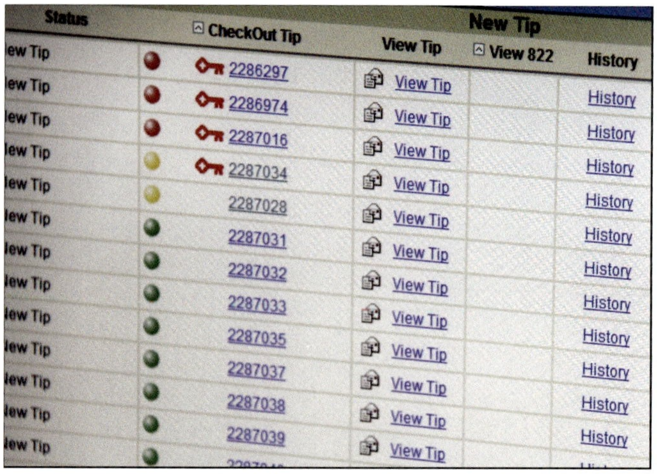

Left: Tips as they appear on a monitor in the Public Access Center Unit.

TO TRACK A THREAT

Inside Our Internet Tip Line

Tip number 2136079 flashed on one of our Submit a Crime Tip computer screens on January 12, eight days before the inauguration of Barack Obama: "I'm going to assassinate the new president of the United States of America," the message said in all capital letters, followed by hundreds of exclamation marks. And there was a P.S.: "YOU HAVE 48 HOURS TO STOP IT FROM HAPPENING...."

Less than 10 minutes later, there was another message from the same person, who called himself Timothy Ryan Gutierrez. He said he had also rigged 40 pounds of C4 and TNT to seven cars outside the Mall of America in Minnesota.

Even before the second message arrived, our **Public Access Center Unit (PACU)**, one of six units in the Counterterrorism Division's National Threat Center Section, which administers the global Internet tip line, had swung into action, working to verify the credibility of the threats and then notifying the Secret Service, our Washington Field Office, our Minneapolis Joint Terrorism Task Force, and other law enforcement agencies. Meanwhile, PACU analysts were helping investigators in the field track the identity and location of the person who sent the messages.

Established immediately after 9/11, the Internet tip line has received more than two million online tips from the public relating to terrorism, counterintelligence, and criminal matters. Unit Chief Jesse Levine said that the main function of the tip line "is to protect against the next September 11," but every tip that comes in is seen by two different analysts, carefully vetted, and acted upon if necessary.

In the early morning hours of January 12, the threat against President-elect Obama's life and the Mall of America submitted by Gutierrez set into motion a whirlwind of activity on the part of the Bureau and our law enforcement partners. In the freezing cold, the vast Mall of America parking lot was swept for bombs. Agents and task force officers from three FBI field offices knocked on doors, trying to determine if Gutierrez was indeed a real person. He was.

In Andrews, Texas, agents found his mother, who said her troubled 21-year-old son was living in Colorado with his brother and working as a welder.

About 12 hours after his e-mail threats arrived on our website, agents knocked on Gutierrez' door in Cortez. After initially denying it, he finally admitted to sending the e-mails. He also reportedly said, "I didn't think you would find me so fast." Gutierrez was later indicted and pled guilty to threatening Obama and transmission of threats in interstate commerce to use explosives. His sentencing is scheduled for next month.

It's not just threats against the president that get attention at PACU, Special Agent Eric Reese, a PACU watch commander, said. "Every piece of information—whether tip or threat—no matter how insignificant it might seem, is carefully scrutinized using all the appropriate open-source and authorized law enforcement data at our disposal."

That scrutiny requires an around-the-clock operation involving three shifts and about 25 Bureau employees who handle more than 900 tips every day of the week. So far this year, PACU has already received more than 160,000 tips—and each one is considered serious until proven otherwise.

"I think the most important thing for the public to remember is that every single piece of information submitted to the tip line is reviewed by FBI personnel," Reese said. If you consider the magnitude of 9/11 and the threats that still remain to the homeland, he added, "there is too much at stake to leave anything to chance."

ONLINE AUCTION FRAUD

Don't Let it Happen to You

Computers, sports memorabilia, rare coins, designer fashions, and even cars.

These are just a few of the items offered for sale every day on legitimate online auction sites. They're also just a small sample of the items used to lure unsuspecting victims into online auction fraud schemes.

Most of the one million-plus transactions that take place each day on these websites are legitimate; just a fraction actually result in some type of fraud.

But even that fraction adds up. According to the latest report of the Internet Crime Complaint Center (IC3), more than 70,000 complaints made to IC3 last year—about one in every four—involved online auction scams.

There are a variety of auction frauds, but here are some of the more common ones to watch out for:

- **Overpayment fraud** targets the seller. A seller advertises a high-value item—like a car or a computer—on the Internet. A scammer contacts the seller to purchase the item, then sends the seller a counterfeit check or money order for an amount greater than the price of the item. The purchaser asks the seller to deposit the payment, deduct the actual sale price, and then return the difference to the purchaser.
- **Wire transfer schemes** start with fraudulent and misleading ads for the sale of high-value items being posted on well-known online auction sites. When buyers take the bait, they are directed to wire money to the crooks using a money transfer company. Once the money changes hands, the buyer never hears from them again.
- **Second-chance schemes** involve scammers who offer losing bidders of legitimate auctions the opportunity to buy the item(s) they wanted at reduced prices. They usually require that victims send payment through money transfer companies, but then don't follow through on delivery.

And needless to say, in all of these schemes customers never get what they pay for.

Who is behind the scams. Mostly individuals. However, there are exceptions: criminal enterprises from West Africa are especially fond of the overpayment scams, while Romanian crime groups favor the second-chance schemes.

One in four complaints in 2008 to the Internet Crime Complaint Center involved online auction fraud.

We're working to address the problem. We've had a number of successful auction fraud investigations, worked collaboratively with other agencies, including one in Virginia and one in Texas.

What to do if you've been victimized. Go to the Internet Crime Complaint Center or the Federal Trade Commission websites and submit a complaint. The more we know about the extent of the crime—including the specific methods being used to perpetrate it—the more effective we can be in preventing and investigating these scams. You can also report incidents to your local police and to auction companies.

So, how can you avoid being a victim of auction fraud? A few tips:

- Ask the seller for a phone number and verify it.
- Beware of buyers who insist on wire transfers as the only form of payment they'll accept.
- For big-ticket items, use a legitimate online escrow service that will hold the payment until you receive what you've ordered.
- If you receive an overpayment as a seller, don't cash it but instead ask for the exact purchase price.
- Don't ever give out your social security or driver's license number—a legitimate seller wouldn't ask.
- Be skeptical if the price sounds too low.

Left: My Harrison, special agent in charge of the Memphis Field Office, speaks to young girls at the juvenile detention center in Memphis, Tennessee.

POSITIVE ROLE MODELS

Memphis Agents Help At-Risk Children

The teenagers were all dressed in orange jumpsuits —standard attire at the juvenile detention center in Memphis, Tennessee. They were sitting in a windowless room, listening to FBI Special Agent in Charge My Harrison talk about turning their young lives around.

Some of these offenders—boys and girls ranging in age from 18 to as young as 9—are charged with serious crimes, including assaults, carjackings, and even murder.

"Seeing successful people, especially ones who had a difficult start in life, can have a positive effect on these children," said Harrison, who heads our Memphis Field Office. "Many of them have never seen an FBI agent before we walk through the door."

Judy McEwen, administrator for the Juvenile Court of Memphis and Shelby County, runs the state grant program that brings volunteer leaders from the community to the detention center to talk with the young offenders. Most of the children are held there for only a few days—they have a court date to determine the disposition of their case, after which they could be transferred to adult court, a juvenile facility, or be sent home to their parents. "While we have them here," McEwen said, "we want to do something good with them."

The grant program is called GOAL—Greater Opportunities for Additional Learning—and Harrison, along with other agents and staff from our Memphis office, are happy to participate.

"My message is simple," Harrison said: "Just because you're here today doesn't mean you have to be here for the rest of your life." Her words hold a special meaning when she tells her personal story.

Harrison grew up "very poor" and on welfare in the housing projects of Tampa, Florida. She and her siblings "could have gone one way or the other," she said. But she was determined to better herself, and people helped her along the way. Harrison eventually graduated from college—she and her mother attended together—and realized her goal of becoming a police officer. She later joined the Bureau and has been special agent in charge of the Memphis office for the past four years.

"I could not have done this alone," she said. "Growing up, people helped me." And now it's her turn to give back—to let at-risk children know they, too, can set goals and achieve them.

The FBI has a number of programs aimed at young people, including Junior Special Agents in Training and the Adopt-a-School Program. But GOAL—while not specifically a Bureau program—is different because it reaches out to troubled youth who are already in the court system.

"We want to instill something positive in their minds," said Sheila Mosby, our community outreach coordinator in Memphis, who also participates in the GOAL program. "Right now their actions are leading to nowhere, and it doesn't have to be like that."

"Obviously we can't reach all of these children," Harrison said. "But if you can help just one, then that's a good day."

Program administrator McEwen sums it up this way: "A lot of these kids do not have hope for a brighter future, and this program provides hope. That's one of the things each speaker leaves them with—the idea that they can change."

BODIES OF EVIDENCE
Part 1: FBI Trains at Body Farm

The bug expert gathered FBI agents around the table to introduce his maggots. He selected a mature one from a watery dish and held it up to his eyepiece, staring through its translucent carapace like a jeweler appraising a precious stone.

"All of these, if you look, have a gut in them," said Dr. Ian Dadour, a forensic entomologist, explaining how pinpointing a maggot's age can tell a lot about what it's eating. "So this means they're still feeding…they haven't used all their food up."

Welcome to Day Two of the FBI Recovery of Human Remains course, an annual week-long field study for 40 special agents and professionals who are Evidence Response Team members in field offices around the country. The popular course, held each May at the "Body Farm" at the University of Tennessee in Knoxville, pairs teams of agents with leading forensic anthropologists to learn how to best identify and excavate human remains to preserve the many clues and pieces of evidence that decaying bodies may leave behind.

Day One is classroom instruction and lectures from experts in the field, including Dr. William M. Bass, who in 1981 created the Anthropological Research Facility, or Body Farm, on a wooded hillside behind the University of Tennessee Medical Center. There, some 70 bodies that were left to science are laid out in various states of repose—buried, exposed, entombed. Bass began the venture as a novel way to study human decomposition and insect activity, but it has evolved into an important teaching environment.

"The initial use of the facility as a training classroom began with the Bureau," said Dr. Murray K. Marks, a forensic anthropologist and protégé of Dr. Bass who helps run the FBI course. In fact, it was in 1999 that the FBI, after participating in several large-scale body recovery operations overseas, linked up with the Body Farm to get expert instruction on human remains recovery.

In addition to the maggot lesson on Day Two, agents learn the technical aspects of what is essentially an archeological dig—probing for loose soil, measuring datum points, and the painstaking work of removing soil by hand. On the morning of **Day Three**, the agents don protective Tyvek suits, rubber gloves, and boots and divide into teams. Their task over the next two days: find a buried body, excavate it, and see what clues emerge.

A student excavates a shallow grave at the Body Farm in Knoxville, Tennessee.

"We don't go in with mechanical equipment or even shovels," said Special Agent Gary Reinecke of the Evidence Response Team Unit at the FBI Laboratory in Quantico, Virginia. Reinecke's experience digging up evidence of war crimes in Kosovo led, in part, to the human remains course. The work is slow and methodical to preserve potential evidence. "They'll be on their hands and knees with hand trowels and other small tools, brushes, and eventually they'll find the remains."

Later in this series, we follow agents as they hone their forensic skills and unearth bodies of evidence in the storied environs of the Body Farm.

One agent offers a preview: "I definitely don't think anyone could just walk in here and deal with the smell and also the sight of a human being decomposing," said Medora Arnaud, a field photographer in our Houston office. "But you know you have a job to do. And I'm sure a lot of times that's what gets a lot of people through it."

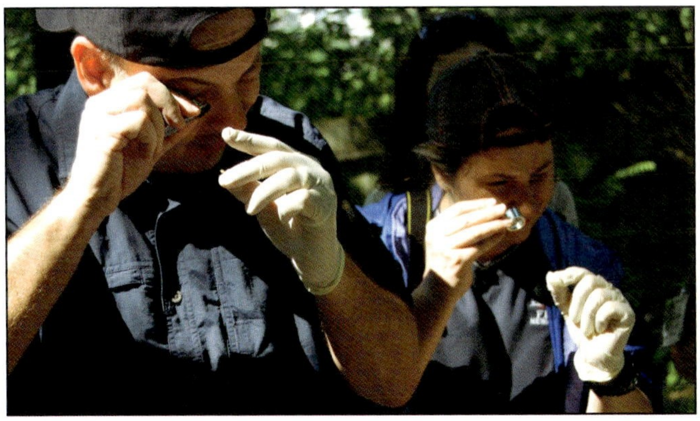

Students inspect maggots to determine their age.

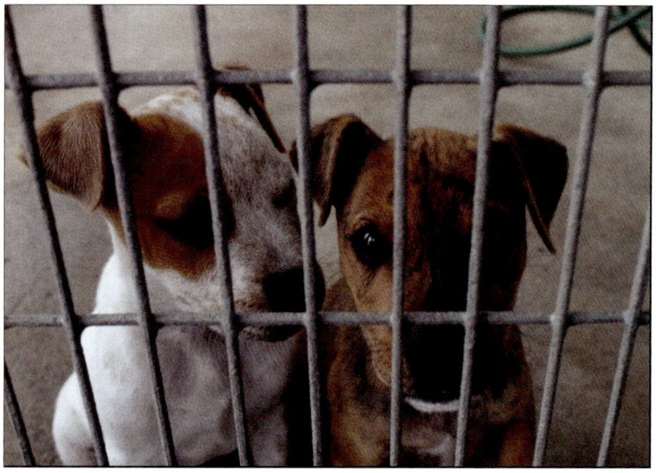

Left: FBI agents helped bust the largest dog fighting operation ever seen in the U.S. Stock photo.

CANINE CRUELTY

Five-State Dog Fighting Ring Busted

A year-long investigation by federal, state, and local law enforcement agencies has resulted in the arrests of approximately 30 people across five states in what officials are calling the largest dog fighting operation ever seen in the U.S.

In addition to the arrests, about 350 dogs—mostly pit bull terriers—were seized during early-morning raids yesterday in Missouri, Texas, Illinois, Iowa, and Oklahoma and will be cared for by local humane societies. Those arrested for their involvement face felony charges that carry maximum sentences of five years in prison and fines of up to $250,000.

"Forcing a dog to fight to its death is not a sport," said John Gillies, special agent in charge of our St. Louis office. The FBI played a significant role in the multi-agency investigation that in the Eastern District of Missouri resulted in the arrests of five men and the seizure of more than 150 dogs at a variety of dog fighting locations. "There is nothing respectable about encouraging two animals to torture and dismember each other," Gillies said.

The U.S. Department of Agriculture's Office of Inspector General headed the investigation, and our St. Louis office was involved from start to finish. "This was a criminal enterprise," said one of our agents there. "It involved illegal drugs given to the dogs and also money laundering from wagering that took place at the dog fights."

According to the indictments, the defendants acquired, bred, and trained pit bull dogs for the purpose of fighting. The defendants denied the dogs adequate medical treatment as a result of injuries suffered after the fights, and they "routinely" destroyed dogs—sometimes by electrocution—that became severely injured after fighting.

In Kansas City, Missouri, defendants allegedly constructed fighting pits for the dog fights, were timekeepers and referees during the fights, and placed wagers on the outcomes. The fights were often so violent and bloody that some of the defendants were designated as "sponge men"—they provided sponges to the dogs' handlers to wipe blood from their dogs or to cool them down during the fight.

After a set of fights last April, the indictment says, one of the defendants used a .22-caliber rifle to shoot and kill two dogs who fought but didn't perform up to his expectations. The dogs were shot in the head twice, then placed in plastic containers outside the garage where the fights had taken place.

Thanks to a 2007 federal law championed by animal welfare organizations, dog fighting is banned throughout the country and is a felony in all 50 states.

"Dog fighting is an illegal and despicable practice," our agent in St. Louis said. "We are very pleased with the outcome of the investigation and the way our law enforcement partners worked together."

A DANGEROUS BETRAYAL

The Case of the Cash Hungry Contractor

Two hundred thousand dollars—not a huge sum of money in return for betraying one's country. But that's exactly how much money Roy Lynn Oakley asked for when he attempted to sell stolen parts of uranium enrichment equipment to someone he thought was an agent of a foreign government.

Oakley's contact was an "agent" all right, but not from a foreign country—it was an undercover agent from the FBI.

How it all began. In January 2007, our Knoxville office learned that Oakley—an employee of the East Tennessee Technology Park in Oak Ridge—was trying to sell restricted U.S. Department of Energy (DOE) materials.

The East Tennessee Technology Park was formerly known as the K-25 building, a DOE facility that opened during the 1940s and produced highly enriched uranium used in the manufacture of atomic weapons. DOE later shut down the facility and contracted with a company—Bechtel Jacobs—to dismantle and demolish the plant. Oakley was an employee of Bechtel Jacobs.

Working with DOE's Office of Counterintelligence, we used sophisticated investigative techniques, interviews, and analysis of records to further pinpoint Oakley as a suspect.

The next phase. To catch Oakley in the act, we began an undercover operation. Our agent contacted Oakley and told him he was representing a foreign government and had heard that Oakley was offering to sell some classified materials. During recorded phone calls, Oakley said he had stolen parts of the uranium enrichment fuel rods and other related hardware items from his place of employment that he was willing to sell for $200,000.

Our undercover agent eventually agreed to the deal, and a face-to-face meeting was set up for January 26, 2007. Both parties showed up at the meeting place, money and classified components were exchanged, and Oakley was ultimately arrested and charged with violating the Atomic Energy Act of 1954.

The East Tennessee Technology Park. Courtesy of the Department of Energy.

Oakley's confession. So why did he do it? Not because of any anti-U.S. ideology. Not because he was angry at his employer. No, he did it purely for the money. Oakley wanted to retire from Bechtel during 2007 but was deep in debt and needed cash.

He told us he took the materials home with him and kept them in a metal box…until he could find a buyer.

In January 2009, Oakley pled guilty to trying to sell these materials. He admitted that he knew the items were "restricted" and that they play a crucial role in the production of highly enriched uranium which is used for atomic weapons (through what's called the gaseous diffusion process). In June, he was sentenced in U.S. District Court in Knoxville to six years in prison.

Upon Oakley's sentencing, Knoxville Special Agent in Charge Rick Lambert said, "Bringing to justice the trusted insider who would betray America for private gain remains the FBI's highest priority."

Left: Students in the FBI course use hand tools during excavation to protect bones and other artifacts a gravesite might yield.

BODIES OF EVIDENCE

Part 2: 'Scraping the Layers Away'

It's a balmy Wednesday morning in the parking lot outside the "Body Farm," a two-plus-acre wooded landscape where the science of human decomposition is on vivid display.

It's Day Three of the FBI's annual Recovery of Human Remains course. And the students, 40 FBI Evidence Response Team members, are finally going to get their hands dirty after two days of intense coursework.

As they duct tape themselves into Tyvek body suits and rubber gloves, the morning air is ripe with the sweet aroma of bug spray and sunscreen, punctuated occasionally by a pungent whiff of what's to come over the next two days. Most here have already worked cases recovering human remains. This course—led by some of the nation's leading forensic anthropologists—provides a more scientific foundation for approaching a scene, recording it, and excavating it to elicit the most evidence.

"The fundamental truth about excavation is it can only be done once," says Dr. Stanley Rhine, a forensic anthropologist and professor emeritus at the University of New Mexico who was among the course's instructors and team leaders.

The class is divided into six teams that will venture into the woods to locate "clandestine burials," careful to avoid disturbing the dozens of exposed corpses that make up the University of Tennessee's Anthropological Research Facility, or Body Farm. The teams will look for visual clues that betray recent burials, such as subtle changes in soil color or vegetation. Then they will gently poke long probes into the clay to see how easily the soil gives way.

The students follow rigid archeological protocols, flagging potential burial sites and then roping them off into staked grids for an orderly excavation. By early afternoon, the teams have identified sites and settled into the painstaking—even tedious—job of scraping away layers of soil and screening it for bones or other artifacts.

"We've been working since about 8 o'clock this morning and we're only down into the ground about four inches," says Medora Arnaud, a photographer in our Houston office. "You have to go very slow. You're mainly scraping the layers away to make sure you don't miss anything."

Arnaud is on Dr. Rhine's team, which by day's end appears to be progressing well. A body has been discovered and mostly uncovered—rib cage, arms, one leg exposed. But webs of roots and a piece of lumber wedged in the grave are slowing things down.

The next morning, teams pick up with a few more hours of digging, sketching, and screening before removing the skeletons, which are later cleaned and measured to add to the university's growing body of work.

But there are a few surprises. Dr. Rhine's team discovers a second body in the same grave, just a few inches away from the first. Another team finds a suitcase-sized oval mass of bones and tissue in their excavation, explaining why it was so difficult to pinpoint the bones with probes.

Each of the digs presents unique twists and challenges—true of most Evidence Response Team work and a key teaching point. The work is taxing, even stomach-turning at times. But Dr. Murray K. Marks, one of the course's forensic anthropologists, puts it in perspective.

"It's just like a crime scene," he says. "It isn't about you. It's about the victims or…training the agents that need to go into that scene. You put that first, and you kind of become inconsequential to the mission at hand."

TOP TEN FUGITIVE CAPTURED

Charged with Brutal Attack on Police

Emigdio Preciado, Jr., a career criminal and member of a violent California street gang who was on our Ten Most Wanted Fugitives list for a brutal attack on police officers nine years ago, has been captured in Mexico.

During a routine traffic stop in September 2000, Preciado stepped out of a van and opened fire on two Los Angeles County Sheriff's deputies with an assault rifle. Some 21 rounds were fired, one of them hitting a deputy in the head and critically injuring him.

"When a police officer is shot, our security is threatened," said Sal Hernandez, assistant director in charge of our Los Angeles office, "and it illustrates a brazen attitude that is devoid of respect for the very people society relies upon for protection." During a press conference today, Hernandez added, "This is why this case is so important, and why Preciado's apprehension is so significant."

Preciado—who is believed to be 39 years old and has used nicknames like "Trigger" and "Snyper"—was captured last Friday evening in the hills near Yagos, a rural town in the Mexican state of Nayarit. He had been living there, using the name Regalo Castaneda-Castaneda and was working as a fisherman.

Although his identifying tattoos—the names "Susana" and "Alexa" on his chest—had been surgically removed, Mexican police and our agents present at the arrest conducted fingerprint comparisons and confirmed the fugitive's true identity.

Hernandez said Preciado's capture was the result of "flawless collaboration" between detectives from the Los Angeles Sheriff's Department, our agents, and members of the FBI's Fugitive Task Force in Los Angeles—which includes the Los Angeles Police Department and the Department of Corrections—along with police in Mexico and agents assigned to the U.S. Embassy there.

Although he could not comment on specific details surrounding Preciado's capture, Hernandez said that a reward of $150,000—advertised on our website—will be paid, and "the significance of the publicity in this case, and the reward offered, cannot be overstated."

Emigdio Preciado Jr., one of the FBI's Ten Most Wanted Fugitives, has been apprehended.

Preciado, a U.S. citizen, is currently in the custody of Mexican federal police and is expected to be transferred to Mexico City, where extradition proceedings will take place.

At the time of the shooting in 2000, Preciado was wanted on a California parole violation. He has an extensive criminal history, including arrests for murder, robbery, and narcotics offenses.

Attending today's press conference were the two deputies—Michael Schaap and David Timberlake—who came under fire during Preciado's attack. Timberlake was not hurt in the shooting, and Schaap, who was severely injured, has recovered and returned to duty.

A few facts about our Ten Most Wanted Fugitives program:

- Launched on March 14, 1950;
- 491 fugitives added to the list so far;
- 461 captured (nearly 94 percent success rate);
- Fourteen fugitives apprehended in Mexico, the most of any country outside the U.S.;
- Nearly one third (151) located through citizen cooperation.

THE TOP TEN DILLINGER MYTHS

The Year of the Gangster, Part 4

On July 22, 1934—75 years ago today—Bureau agents put an end to John Dillinger's reign of crime when he was shot and killed near the Biograph Theater in Chicago. Dillinger's story has been told and retold ever since—including in a recent Hollywood movie. Along the way, fact and fiction have often been blended together. Here, from our perspective, are the top ten myths surrounding Dillinger and the facts as we know them.

Myth #10: Dillinger was a "Robin Hood" type criminal, a romantic outlaw.

Dillinger certainly had charm and charisma, but he was no champion of the poor or harmless thief—he was a hardened and vicious criminal. Dillinger stormed police stations in search of weapons and bulletproof vests. He robbed banks and stole cars. He shot at police officers (and may have killed one) and regularly used innocent bystanders as human shields to escape the law. Worse yet, he stood by as his ruthless gang members shot and killed people, including law enforcement officials. And what of his ill-gotten gains? They were used to line his own pockets and those of his partners in crime, not those of impoverished Americans in the midst of the Great Depression.

Myth #9: Dillinger was not carrying a gun the night he was killed.

Dillinger did have a gun on him—a .380 Colt automatic with the serial number scratched out. He reached for that gun when Bureau agents cornered him that fateful night.

Left: The Biograph Theater in Chicago shortly after Dillinger was killed.

Not taking any chances, agents shot him before he had the chance to open fire.

Myth #8: John Dillinger was not killed at the Biograph Theater, a stand-in was.

If this sounds like a conspiracy theory, that's because it is. Claims that a man resembling Dillinger was actually killed have been advanced with only circumstantial evidence. On the other hand, a wealth of information supports Dillinger's demise. Special Agents M. Chaffetz and Earle Richmond, for example, took two sets of fingerprints from the body outside the Biograph Theater, and both were a positive match. Another set taken during the autopsy were also a match

Myth #7: The FBI beat up Evelyn Frechette after her arrest.

Not so. Evelyn "Billie" Frechette—Dillinger's one time girlfriend—was captured on April 9, 1934 and detained in our Chicago Field Office. She was interrogated about Dillinger around the clock for two days under hot lights. She refused to cooperate and was transferred to St. Paul to stand trial for harboring Dillinger. While her interrogation wasn't exactly a walk in the park, at no time did agents attack or strike her. Frechette and her lawyer claimed we did during the trail—most likely to win sympathy.

Myth #6: The FBI took physical specimens from Dillinger's corpse.

There is no evidence suggesting that the Bureau kept "souvenirs" from Dillinger's body or in any way desecrated his remains. According to media reports, however, the local coroner later admitted taking pieces of Dillinger's brain to examine.

Myth #5: East Chicago, Indiana Police killed Dillinger, not FBI agents.

While East Chicago Police officers were instrumental in helping the Bureau track down Dillinger the night he died, they were not in a position to shoot him. According to the drawn-up plans of the takedown and individual testimony, all of these officers were too far away to have an unobstructed shot. The closest—Captain Timothy O'Neil—was stationed across the street; his line of fire would have been blocked by special agents and civilians. In the end, it was Bureau agents who shot and killed Dillinger. Claims that someone else pulled the trigger came much later.

Dillinger's Partners in Crime

These are some of the men who worked with Dillinger at various points in his criminal career.

Myth #4: J. Edgar Hoover hired a bunch of killers to go after Dillinger.

Capturing John Dillinger was certainly the Bureau's top priority in the summer of 1934, but we did not take a "dead or alive" approach as evidenced in our records and in later agent recollections. After the failed raid at Little Bohemia, we did hire several exceptional lawmen with firearms experience and steady gun-hands during times of danger, but only one ended up firing on Dillinger. The idea was to bring in professionals to help mentor less experienced agents, not to get Dillinger at all costs.

Myth #3: Chicago Special Agent in Charge Melvin Purvis single-handedly brought down Dillinger.

Purvis was a key figure, but he definitely did not shoot Dillinger (as some press accounts claimed) and his role in the final days of the case has often been overstated. After the Little Bohemia incident, Director J. Edgar Hoover appointed Inspector and Special Agent Samuel Cowley to oversee what had become a multi-state search. Cowley operated independently, but largely out of our Chicago office. FBI records suggest that he and Purvis worked together on the Dillinger investigation, but Cowley was clearly in charge until the end.

Myth #2: A "lady in a red dress" betrayed Dillinger.

Actually, it was a lady in an orange skirt and white blouse named Anna (Ana) Sage. Sage—a Romanian who was friends with Dillinger's girlfriend at the time, Polly Hamilton—came up with the idea of turning in the fugitive after she was invited to go to the movies with the couple. She contacted the East Chicago, Indiana Police Department, who passed her on to Purvis. While Sage hoped that the FBI might help her avoid deportation, she also wanted the $5,000 reward. She told Purvis she would be attending a movie with Dillinger and Hamilton at the Biograph and would wear an orange skirt to set her apart from the crowd. (The red dress was an invention of the media—red tends to be a more alluring color and apparently sounded better in a headline.) After Dillinger's death, Sage was paid the reward, but the FBI was not able to influence her deportation proceedings, and she was sent back to Romania.

Myth #1: Dillinger died expressing his love for Billie Frechette.

Popular culture likes to play up the "eternal romance" between Dillinger and Frechette, but evidence shows that they were in love only a short time. After Frechette was captured, Dillinger looked elsewhere for romance. He found it with Polly Hamilton—the woman he took to the movies the night he was killed. When he was shot, Dillinger had on him a gold ring inscribed with the words, "With all my love, Polly," as well as a pocket watch that contained a picture of her. Dillinger is thought by some to have whispered something about Billie Frechette as he lay on the sidewalk dying. Several eyewitnesses said they saw Dillinger's lips moving moments before he died, but no one was close enough to hear if he was whispering or simply exhaling for the last time.

Left: FBI agents in Newark lead arrested suspects in the corruption probe onto a bus. AP Photo.

MASSIVE CORRUPTION BUST

Mayors, Rabbis, Politicians, and More

As the buses pulled up to our Newark office yesterday morning carrying 44 prominent political and religious leaders—including mayors, assemblymen, and rabbis—it would have been easy to mistake them as a group of visiting VIPs.

Instead, they were the defendants in a two-track criminal investigation, arrested by our agents during an early morning sweep and charged with political corruption and high-volume international money laundering.

"The list of names and titles of those arrested today sounds like a roster for a community leaders meeting," said Weysan Dun, special agent in charge of our Newark office. "Sadly, these prominent individuals were not in a meeting room but were in the FBI booking room."

Three New Jersey mayors, two state legislators, numerous political operatives, and five well-known rabbis from New York and New Jersey were among those arrested. Charges include politicians accepting cash bribes and rabbis laundering millions of dollars through their tax-exempt charitable organizations. One defendant allegedly conspired to broker the sale of a human kidney for a transplant at a cost of $160,000.

With the assistance of a cooperating witness, we infiltrated a money laundering network that operated internationally between New York, New Jersey, and Israel and laundered tens of millions of dollars through charitable non-profit groups controlled by the rabbis.

In one method of laundering, our undercover witness would write a check to the rabbi's charitable organization—anywhere from tens of thousands of dollars to more than $150,000—and the rabbi would then return the amount of the check in cash, less a 10 percent cut for himself. Defendants in Israel provided large sums of cash for these transactions. The money was kept in "cash houses" in Brooklyn.

When our witness was later introduced to a Jersey City public official, it led to the discovery of a network of corruption that became the second phase of our investigation.

Among those arrested:

- The newly elected mayor of Hoboken, charged with accepting $25,000 in cash bribes, including $10,000 last week from an undercover cooperating witness.
- A New Jersey assemblyman and recent mayoral candidate in Jersey City, charged with taking $15,000 in bribes to help get approvals from high-level state officials for building projects.
- The chief rabbi of a synagogue in Brooklyn, charged with laundering proceeds derived from criminal activity.

Most of the defendants were arrested by agents from our Newark office and from the Internal Revenue Service, who were working in collaboration with the U.S. Attorney's Office in New Jersey. Search warrants were executed at approximately 20 locations in the region to recover large sums of cash and other evidence. The investigation produced hundreds of hours of video and audio recordings documenting much of the money laundering and bribe-taking.

At a press conference yesterday in Newark, Special Agent in Charge Dun said of the arrests, "We hope that our actions today will be the clarion call that prompts significant change in the way business and politics are conducted in the state of New Jersey. Those who engage in this culture of corruption should know the cross hairs of justice will continue to be focused on them."

TERRORISM TAKEDOWN

Seven Charged in North Carolina

FBI agents this morning arrested a group of homegrown terrorists in North Carolina who were heavily armed, organized, and making plans to wage jihad overseas.

The seven men arrested—including a father and his two sons—were charged with providing material support to terrorists and conspiring to murder, kidnap, maim, and injure people overseas.

The father, Daniel Patrick Boyd, once fought in Afghanistan and trained in terrorist camps in Pakistan and Afghanistan. All of the defendants are North Carolina residents, and all but one are U.S. citizens.

"The threat that terrorists and extremists pose to America and our allies has not dulled or gone away," said Owen D. Harris, special agent in charge of the FBI's Charlotte Division. "These arrests today show there are people living among us, in our communities in North Carolina and around the U.S., that are honing their skills to carry out acts of murder and mayhem."

The seven-count indictment details a conspiracy that began in earnest in 2006 and continued until shortly before today's arrests. The defendants trained in the U.S. for battle and were willing to die as martyrs. They raised money to support their training and in some cases recruited and radicalized others to further their cause overseas. In one case, Daniel Patrick Boyd traveled in March 2006 with one of his sons to Gaza to introduce him to individuals who believed violent jihad was a religious obligation. A year later, Boyd and several of the defendants went to Israel to wage jihad but returned without success.

The defendants, as well as some of the additional charges they face, are:

- **Daniel Patrick Boyd**: The 39-year-old Boyd faces charges of possessing a firearm in furtherance of a crime, receiving a firearm through interstate commerce, and also selling a firearm to a felon.
- **Dylan Boyd**: One of Daniel Boyd's sons, Dylan, 22, is also charged with selling a firearm—a 9mm Beretta handgun—to a felon.
- **Zakariya Boyd**: Also a son of Daniel Boyd, Zakariya, 20, is charged with possession of a firearm in furtherance of a crime.

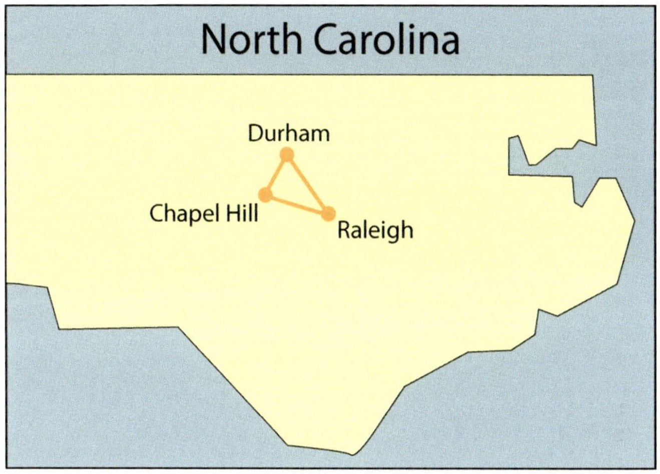

The operation was dubbed "Triangle Terror Takedown" as a geographic reference to the Raleigh, Durham, and Chapel Hill areas of North Carolina.

- **Hysen Sherifi**: The 24-year-old Kosovo native is a legal U.S. resident. As part of the conspiracy, the indictment alleges he traveled to Kosovo in July 2008 to engage in violent jihad, then returned in April to raise support for the mujahedeen. Sherifi allegedly supplied $500 to help fund Daniel Boyd's overseas efforts.
- **Anes Subasic**: The 33-year-old naturalized U.S. citizen discussed preparations with Daniel Boyd to send two people overseas.
- **Mohammad Omar Aly Hassan**: A 22-year-old U.S. citizen.
- **Ziyad Yaghi**: The 21-year-old U.S. citizen traveled to Jordan in October 2006 to engage in violent jihad.

The indictment details the arsenal the defendants built up over several years, including handguns, assault rifles, and a Bushmaster M4A3 that Daniel Boyd allegedly received illegally in 2006. Over the past two months, the defendants practiced with the weapons and developed their military tactics on private property in rural Caswell County.

The Raleigh Joint Terrorism Task Force of the FBI Charlotte Division led the multi-year, multi-agency investigation, dubbed "Triangle Terror Takedown," along with the North Carolina Information Sharing and Analysis Center.

"We will remain vigilant, so must the public," Special Agent in Charge Harris said. "If you see or hear something, act. Call your local police department or the FBI."

CONSUMER ALERT

Online Rental Ads Could be Phony

You can't believe your good fortune—you find a rental home in a nice area through a Craigslist classified ad at an unbelievably low rate. The landlord—who had to leave the country and travel to Nigeria—asks that you wire him two months' worth of rent. You arrive at the home on the agreed-upon date, but there's just one small problem—the house is not actually for rent and its owners know nothing about your agreement.

This latest scam being perpetrated by Nigerian criminals located halfway around the world has been seen in a number of U.S. states, perhaps in response to the current housing market—with fewer people buying, more people are renting.

But it's not really a new scam, just a variation of an old one. The so-called 419 scheme—named after the Nigerian penal code section under which this particular kind of fraud is prosecuted—has been around since the early 1980s. The common thread running through these kinds of scams? The victims are solicited by Nigerian criminals to transfer money out of the U.S. and into the criminals' pockets...usually by being promised something in return. And these schemes *are* profitable, costing victims millions of dollars annually.

In South Carolina, the rental scam problem has become so prevalent that Columbia FBI Special Agent in Charge David Thomas recently issued a warning about it to homeowners and prospective renters, particularly in the Charleston, Columbia, and Hilton Head areas. The scam has also ensnared victims in Rhode Island, Illinois, Colorado, and California, among other states.

How exactly does the rental housing scam work? The criminals search websites that list homes for sale. They take the information in those ads—lock, stock, and barrel—and post it, with their own e-mail address, in an ad on Craigslist (without Craigslist's consent or knowledge) under the housing rentals category. To sweeten the pot, the houses are almost always listed with below-market rental rates.

An interested party will contact the "homeowner" via e-mail, who usually explains that he or she had to leave the U.S. quickly because of some missionary or contract work in Africa. Victims are usually instructed to send money overseas—enough to cover the first and last month's rent—via a wire transfer service (because the crooks know it can't be traced once it gets picked up on the other end).

Renters might sometimes be asked to fill out credit applications asking for personal information like credit history, social security numbers, and work history. The Nigerian crooks can then use this info to commit identity fraud and steal even more money from their victims.

How to avoid being victimized:

- Only deal with landlords or renters who are local;
- Be suspicious if you're asked to only use a wire transfer service;
- Beware of e-mail correspondence from the "landlord" that's written in poor or broken English;
- Research the average rental rates in that area and be suspicious if the rate is significantly lower; and
- Don't give out personal information, like social security, bank account, or credit card numbers.

If you suspect a scam, have already been victimized, or know someone who has fallen victim to a scam, please report it to our Internet Crime Complaint Center to help us determine the extent of the problem.

CUTTING-EDGE TECHNOLOGY

New Ways to Analyze Digital Intel

When our agents are on the trail of suspected terrorists, with appropriate legal approval they can gain access to suspects' e-mail, telephone calls, text messages, and even computer hard drives.

But after we collect what can amount to millions of pieces of digital data, what happens next? How can all that raw intelligence be organized, analyzed, and shared to help stop a terrorist plot before it's too late?

The answer to those questions can be found within our Special Technologies & Applications Office (STAO). In the high stakes arena of national security, STAO is one of our most technologically advanced players. Using custom-designed tools and applications that are so innovative they are sometimes beyond state of the art, STAO's specialty is teasing out critical information—a hidden video file on a hard drive, a key connection among tens of thousands of e-mails—from almost any form of electronic media. Where digital evidence is concerned, STAO Section Chief Christopher "Todd" Doss explained, "We find the needle in the haystack."

Created in the late 1990s and dramatically enhanced as a result of 9/11, the office consists of more than 200 people with expertise in various digital disciplines. And in addition to Bureau personnel, the team collaborates with some of the brightest computer scientists from private industry, academia, and other government agencies.

The primary goal of STAO is to provide investigators with tools to manage and analyze large volumes of digital intelligence and to "cross-correlate" that information so it's available not only to FBI personnel all over the world but also to our partners in the law enforcement and intelligence communities. Is a piece of data from a cell phone in Southeast Asia linked to a terrorism case in Seattle? STAO applications can help connect the dots.

Some of STAO's capabilities include:

- **Visual Analysis.** Finding patterns among enormous amounts of related data exchanged among suspects is a huge challenge. Instead of wading through vast lists of such data in a traditional text-based way, such as in a spreadsheet, STAO created a visual solution called FANTOM that allows agents and analysts to examine connections visually in three dimensions.

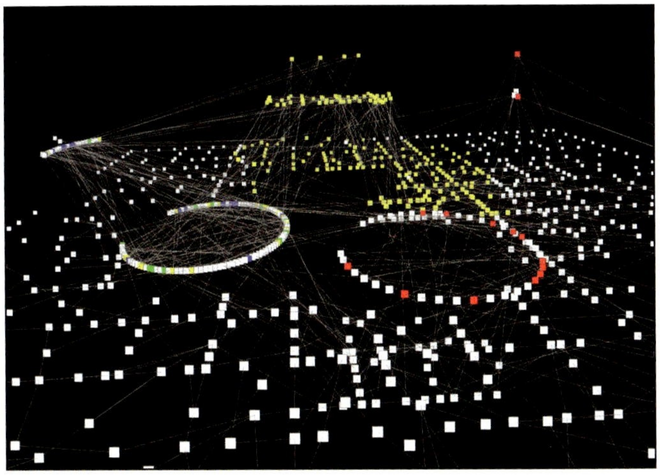

STAO created a cutting-edge visual solution called FANTOM that allows agents and analysts to examine connections visually in three dimensions.

  Each data relationship of a suspect is represented on a large computer monitor by a single point, or "node." Lines, or "edges," between nodes indicate one or more communications made between suspects using a particular method. Using FANTOM, agents can easily find answers to important questions—"Which nodes were most active and most central to all the communications?" "What communications were made at a particular date and time?" Or, "If two suspects exchanged text messages before planting an IED, who else were they texting?" This cutting-edge visual application enables the kind of interactive computing that can provide vital intelligence to investigators.

- **Malicious code analysis.** STAO's experts on malicious software—malware—work closely with our Cyber Division on matters including computer intrusions. These experts are often called upon to testify in child pornography cases when defendants claim that a computer virus was responsible for downloading child porn on their computers. "We can tell if that was indeed the case," an agent explained.

- **Data management.** STAO maintains powerful, easy-to-use systems that can store seized digital files including text, audio, video, and photos. Approved users can search, filter, and share case information with others in the intelligence community—an invaluable tool in our fight against terrorism.

"The bottom line," said one STAO official, "is that our office helps the Bureau and others do their jobs. And whenever we can help catch the bad guy on the criminal side, or provide intelligence on the counterterrorism side, that's what we're here for."

CAMPUS PUBLIC SAFETY

Our Post-9/11 Role

Think about how much there is to protect: our nation's bright young minds and future leaders, all the capabilities and intellectual assets of our higher institutions of learning, the innovative (and often proprietary) research that takes place on campus and helps fuel the economy, the high-profile speakers and huge sporting venues.

Then factor in the realities of a post-9/11 world.

This is why the FBI takes campus public safety more seriously than ever. Our role is a supporting one—we work closely with the approximately 30,000 campus public safety officers who work diligently to protect the 4,200 colleges and universities across the country. In addition to this partnership with the college and university law enforcement community, we also partner with the leaders of these institutions.

A few examples of the partnerships we've put in place in recent years:

...Our **Joint Terrorism Task Force (JTTF) Campus Liaison Initiative** designates an FBI agent or task force officer from every field office to coordinate with campus public safety officers and other school personnel—with the overriding goal of addressing terror threats and preventing attacks. Our JTTF agents reach out regularly to campus police and school administrators—sharing threat information, offering presentations, providing training and lists of threat indicators, etc. About 20 campus public safety officers are full-fledged JTTF members—we're working to increase that number.

...Our **Academic Alliance Program** was set up to tackle national security challenges like global adversaries trying to steal U.S. information or technologies, such as proprietary information and trade secrets. Included in that program are:

- Our **National Security Higher Education Advisory Board** (NSHEAB) is comprised of 20 university and college presidents and chancellors, many from schools with large research labs. The board meets several times a year with us in Washington D.C., often in concert with other federal agencies, to talk about national security implications facing their research facilities.
- On a broader scale, our **College and University Security Effort**, or CAUSE, joins agents in charge of our 56 field offices with heads of local institutions to discuss similar issues brought up at the NSHEAB meetings. Each field office also has a strategic partnership coordinator who—much like the terrorism campus liaison agent—maintains relationships with schools that are members of our InfraGard program.

...Our **Office of Law Enforcement Coordination** (OLEC) was created following 9/11 to build further on our relationships with law enforcement partners at all levels, including campus officers. OLEC has a management program assistant on campus public safety who works directly with national groups like the International Association of Campus Law Enforcement Administrators and the University and College Police Section of the International Association of Chiefs of Police. OLEC helps get local campus law enforcement more of what they need (resources, training, information, etc.) so they can continue to address crimes and national security threats.

Through it all, our job is to help universities thrive and stay safe...while protecting the security of our country overall. Our understanding of the national and international threat picture helps support the local work of campus public safety...and vice versa. It's a partnership that makes sense in our post-9/11 world.

SHARING INTELLIGENCE
To Fight Transnational Gangs

The members of a new international group formed to help fight the violent MS-13 and 18th Street gangs were meeting for the first time last month at the FBI Academy in Quantico, Virginia when the reason for the group's existence became perfectly clear: representatives from El Salvador and Mexico realized they had been tracking the activities of the same MS-13 suspect. Now both countries could benefit from their collective intelligence efforts.

"These gangs are transnational, and right now they pretty much cross our borders for criminal activity at will," said L.T. Chu, an FBI intelligence analyst with our MS-13 National Gang Task Force and the program manager for the new group—the Central American Intelligence Program (CAIP).

The FBI is involved in investigative partnerships to battle transnational gangs, but CAIP, whose members are primarily from Central America, is the first organization to focus exclusively on intelligence.

At the annual Policia Nacional Civil Anti-Gang conference last spring in El Salvador, Chu said, "We determined that one of our weaknesses was exchange of intelligence. We realized that it was crucial that we set up a forum and a mechanism to exchange this information."

That thinking is very much in keeping with the Bureau's overall post 9/11 efforts to become a proactive, intelligence-gathering organization that prevents criminal activity rather than responding to crimes after the fact.

A joint initiative of the FBI and the State Department, CAIP consists of veteran criminal intelligence analysts from the U.S., El Salvador, Honduras, Guatemala, Mexico, and Canada who work gang-related matters. Besides intelligence sharing, the objective is to standardize reports and other intelligence products and to minimize the communication gaps between countries—gaps that currently allow gang members to operate across borders.

At its first meeting—the group will meet three times a year at rotating host countries—interpreters assisted participants who spoke little English or Spanish. But even with the language barrier, everyone understands the significance of CAIP's mission.

Members of the Central American Intelligence Program discuss issues at its inaugural meeting in July.

"Gangs are a huge problem in Guatemala," said Heber Ramirez, chief of intelligence analysis for Policia Nacional Civil de Guatemala. Through an interpreter he explained, "It is very important that we have established relationships with these countries so that we can track gang activities across borders." And as CAIP works toward standardizing how intelligence products are produced, he added, "We will be reporting very specific information in very specific ways that everyone can understand."

Douglas Funes, who heads the transnational gang unit for the Policia Nacional Civil in El Salvador—which includes two embedded FBI agents working gang-related investigations—agreed that CAIP will be a vital weapon in fighting gangs.

El Salvador is "contaminated" by violent gangs, Funes said, and MS-13 alone has some 15,000 members in the country, including many members in the prison population. "Perhaps the most serious problem with MS-13," he added, "is that they are constantly recruiting new members."

"MS-13 and 18th Street are developing constantly and changing their methods," Chu said. "The only way to fight them is to understand their organizations from the top down. And the only way to accomplish that is through cooperative intelligence sharing across borders. That is why CAIP is so important."

BUSINESSES BEWARE
Of Mass Marketing Scams

Almost everyone has heard horror stories about individuals who have been taken in by mass marketing fraud schemes—from phony sweepstakes to lottery scams. But here's something you may not know: the very same fraudsters who target individual consumers also target businesses.

Illicit mass marketers know that the keepers of corporate funds may be just as susceptible to fake ploys as anyone else. And while business-oriented fraud usually results in losses of a few hundreds dollars the first time a company is hit, employees may continue to fall victim to these scams if the company has insufficient internal controls.

So what sort of mass marketing frauds are perpetrated against businesses? Here are just a few examples of what might happen to your companies:

- Masquerading as your usual office supplies provider, a fraudulent mass marketer contacts your employees, offering products at reduced or current prices in anticipation of impending rate increases. After paying the invoice, your company never receives the supplies it purchased.
- Your organization is asked to buy ad space in a business directory. The directory never sees the light of day, or only scammed companies like yours receive a copy.
- Criminals send invoices for unordered or undelivered products showing higher-than-agreed-upon prices, trying to exploit poor communication channels that may exist in your company and hoping that phony invoices will be paid without a second look.
- Your business receives an information packet offering to create and host your website. The packet includes a card that must be returned in order to "opt out" of the service, but the card is simply ignored or thrown out. Your company is then billed for web services it never ordered.
- In a variation of the advance-fee scheme that often targets individual consumers, perpetrators—usually targeting small businesses—offer low interest loans in exchange for an advance fee. You pay the fee, but your business never receives the loan.

While the FBI and other law enforcement agencies vigorously investigate frauds of all kinds, there are steps your businesses can take to protect themselves. For example:

- Educate yourself and your employees—especially frontline and accounts payable and receivable personnel—about common fraud schemes;
- Always ask for offers in writing, and require a written contract or purchase order for ANY transaction;
- Carefully review all invoices and compare them to expense records to make sure they are legitimate (and keep all records!);
- Use a credit card for purchasing supplies and services (if the vendor fails to deliver, you can dispute the charges);
- Don't give out full names of employees, as fraudsters can obtain an employee's name and then later claim this individual authorized the purchase of a product or service; and
- Be wary of accepting checks, because in some cases perpetrators have conducted a series of smaller, legitimate transactions to enhance their credibility and then used a counterfeit check to pay for a large order.

If you suspect you've been scammed, file a complaint with the Federal Trade Commission's Consumer Sentinel, a database accessed by law enforcement agencies around the country. You can also contact your local FBI office.

For more advice on how to protect yourself and your companies from fraud, visit our "Be Crime Smart" website.

COMPUTER FORENSICS LABS

Making a Digital Difference

A domestic terrorist. A kidnapper. A corrupt politician. An identity thief.

These are just of a few of those brought to justice with the help of our Regional Computer Forensics Laboratories (RCFLs), according to the latest RCFL annual report now available online.

Fiscal year (FY) 2008—which ran from October 1, 2007 to September 30, 2008—marked the ninth year for the RCFL program, which had 14 labs operating around the country by the end of the fiscal year. Labs planned in Orange County, California and Albuquerque, New Mexico will soon bring the total to 16.

How does the program work? We provide start-up and operational funding, training, equipment, a director, and a network administrator; state, local, and other federal law enforcement agencies supply forensic examiners to staff the lab.

RCFLs examine digital evidence in all sorts of criminal and national security cases. And the cases come from a variety of law enforcement agencies—at the local, state, and federal level.

Combined, our network of labs racked up some pretty big numbers during the year. The RCFLs and their examiners:

- Processed 1,756 terabytes of data (a single terabyte is equivalent to the content of one large library!);
- Conducted 4,524 forensic examinations;
- Assisted 591 onsite law enforcement operations;
- Trained 4,991 law enforcement officers in digital forensics techniques; and
- Appeared in court 74 times to testify at trial.

And here a few more numbers: RCFL personnel examined 58,609 pieces of digital media of all kinds. The most popular types included CDs and hard drives (about 17,500 each); floppy disks (10,982); DVDs (4,310); flash media (2,548); and cell phones (2,226). Other items included digital cameras, GPS devices, and video and audio tapes.

An examiner from the Heart of America RCFL in Missouri labels a hard drive sent in for inspection.

But even more impressive than these statistical accomplishments were the important investigations these RCFLs supported. For instance:

- The Miami Valley (Ohio) RCFL helped the Columbus Joint Terrorism Task Force investigate Christopher Paul, who eventually pled guilty to conspiring to use a weapon of mass destruction against targets in Europe and the United States.
- The Kentucky RCFL examined media seized during a civil rights investigation into abuses against inmates by Fayette County Detention Center officers.
- The Heart of America (Missouri) RCFL uncovered clues on a computer belonging to Lisa Montgomery, charged with the murder of a 23-year-old pregnant woman and the kidnapping of her unborn child.
- The New Jersey RCFL supported the investigation into corruption charges against former Newark Mayor Sharpe James by examining several computers related to the case.
- The Philadelphia RCFL uncovered documents and spreadsheets detailing the crimes of identify thief Jocelyn Kirsch and her partner, who stole personal information from friends, co-workers, and neighbors.

The number—and storage capacity—of electronic devices seized during investigations continues to grow. During FY 2008, RCFLs processed 27 percent more terabytes of data than they did during FY 2007.

But as the workload grows, so does our commitment to developing effective solutions with our federal, state, and local partners.

TOOLS OF THE TRADE

FBI Dive Team

They work in what is often a dark, difficult environment that requires precision teamwork and equipment that supplies the very air they breathe. They are the members of our Underwater Search Evidence Response Team (USERT), and their efforts to recover a knife, gun, or an airplane's black box can be critical to an investigation.

Using specialized equipment, including sonar, metal detectors, and lift bags capable of raising a two-ton vehicle from the depths, team members working together above and below the surface can locate evidence as large as a jet engine and as small as a bullet buried in underwater dirt.

Facts

Diving with a helmet and other gear, total weight of equipment on the surface can exceed 100 pounds.

USERT members search to recover evidence or work on humanitarian missions. They are not a tactical team, like Navy SEALS.

The team generally follows recreational diving limits, descending no deeper than 130 feet for non-decompression dives.

Despite the usual pitch-black environment they work in, divers rarely use lights below the surface because particulate matter churned up from walking on the bottom diffuses any light. Instead, sonar equipment—usually controlled from the surface—is used to direct the divers and locate evidence.

Divers must be in top physical condition. Walking the bottom with a current of 3 or 4 knots is as physically demanding as jogging on the surface.

Gear

USERT is equipped with a variety of gear, from inflatable boats and larger vessels to underwater robotic vehicles and side-scan sonar units. The most important element to achieving its mission, though, is the teamwork between the divers in the water and the team operating on the surface.

Air Supply

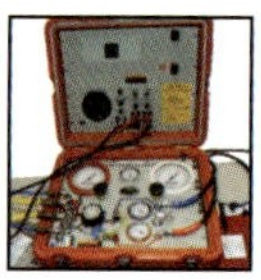

Surface air supply connects to a three-hose, color-coded cord: yellow hose carries air; red hose carries communications wires; blue hose is the pneumofathometer, a depth gauge used so team members on the surface know divers' depths at all times.

Box allows surface team to run air and communications for two divers at one time. Attached speaker system allows for two-way communication between team members above and below the surface.

Blue and orange hoses are connected to tanks on the surface. Potentially unlimited air supply can be achieved by using an air compressor instead of tanks.

Helmet

Kirby Morgan 17B: weighs about 30 pounds, standard commercial diving helmet.

Block (on the right side): allows diver to switch from surface air to emergency gas supply carried in tank on his back.

Block switch: front switch ventilates helmet and prevents deadly carbon dioxide buildup; also functions like a portable air-conditioning unit to cool the diver's face.

Nose piece: allows diver to clear his ears while descending to equalize air pressure in the ear canal.

Regulator: Venturi switch allows adjustment of air intake.

Quad valve exhaust: allows air bubbles to exit the helmet when diver exhales.

Ear speakers: enables communication between surface team and fellow divers.

AGA mask

Full face mask uses positive pressure as opposed to a "demand" regulator.

Most popular mask for commercial and military diving.

Has valsalva capability for equalizing ears during dive.

Two ear buds on either side of the mask allow for communications with other team members.

Built-in snorkel capability for surface work.

Buoyancy

Buoyancy Compression Device (BC): A vest-like device with a wing on the back that can be manually inflated or deflated to control buoyancy; also contains removable weight pouches.

Dry Suit

Vulcanized rubber suit that keeps divers dry. Up to three layers of clothing can be worn underneath, depending on the water temperature and where they are diving. Dry suit seals to helmet for water-tight fit.

Lift Bags

For safety reasons, divers are prohibited from lifting anything above 15 pounds by themselves. Lift bags inflate to lift objects as large as 2,000-pound vehicles. Bags are inflated either by divers or, for larger items, by surface-supplied air.

Search Equipment

Depending on whether the mission is humanitarian—recovering bodies from a plane crash or shipwreck—or to recover evidence such as a weapon, the dive team employs an array of equipment, from metal detectors to underwater remotely operated vehicles.

Sonar

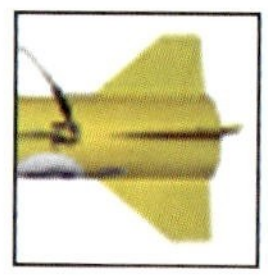

Side scan "Towfish" unit: Torpedo-like sonar designed to be towed behind or alongside a boat to cover wider search areas.

Sector scan sonar on tripod with GPS grid: Provides 360-degree analysis of the bottom composition out to a maximum range of 300 feet.

Self-righting tripod is dropped from the surface; sends signal to computers on the surface; surface team directs the divers where to search.

Transducers send and receive sonar waves.

Boat/ROV

A 27-foot Boston Whaler is the primary dive platform for USERT. It is equipped with a dive door for easy on/off access for divers and has a crane-like device called a davit that allows the boat to winch a large remotely operated vehicle on and off the deck.

Remotely Operated Vehicle (ROV): Units come in various sizes and are generally equipped with thrusters, lights, a camera that can transmit high definition images directly to the surface, and an "articulator" or manipulator that can grab small objects.

A BYTE OUT OF HISTORY

The Case of the Harvey's Casino Bomb

In the early morning hours of August 26, 1980—29 years ago today—men wearing white jumpsuits and pretending to deliver an IBM copy machine rolled a bomb into Harvey's Resort Hotel and Casino in Stateline, Nevada, near Lake Tahoe.

So began one of the most unusual cases in our history.

A note left with the bomb—titled STERN WARNING TO THE MANAGEMENT AND BOMB SQUAD—began ominously: "Do not move or tilt this bomb, because the mechanism controlling the detonators in it will set it off at a movement of less than .01 of the open end Ricter scale."

"Do not try to take it apart," the note went on. "The flathead screws are also attached to triggers and as much as ¼ to ¾ of a turn will cause an explosion. … This bomb is so sensitive that the slightest movement either inside or outside will cause it to explode. This bomb can never be dismantled or disarmed without causing an explosion. Not even by the creator."

The "creator," we later discovered, was 59-year-old John Birges, Sr.—who wanted $3 million in cash in return for supplying directions to disconnect two of the bomb's three automatic timers so it could be moved to a remote area before exploding.

The device—two steel boxes stacked one atop the other—contained nearly 1,000 pounds of dynamite. Inside the resort, Birges made sure the bomb was exactly level, then armed it using at least eight triggering mechanisms.

"We had never seen anything quite like it," said retired Special Agent Chris Ronay, an explosives examiner who was called to the scene along with other experts.

After being discovered, the bomb was photographed, dusted for fingerprints, X-rayed, and studied. Finally, more than 30 hours later, a plan was agreed upon: if the two boxes could be severed using a shaped charge of C4 explosive, it might disconnect the detonator wiring from the dynamite.

Harvey's and other nearby casinos in Lake Tahoe were evacuated, and on the afternoon of August 27, the shaped charge was remotely detonated.

After authorities evacuated Harvey's casino and the surrounding area, experts attempted to disarm the bomb, but their efforts were unsuccessful, and the bomb exploded. Fortunately, no one was killed or injured in the blast.

The plan was the best one available at the time, but it didn't work. The bomb exploded, creating a five-story crater in the hotel. "Looking up from ground level," Ronay said, "you could see TV sets swinging on electric cords and toilets hanging on by pipes. Debris was everywhere." Fortunately, because of the evacuation, no one was killed or injured.

To this day, the Harvey's bomb remains one of the most unique improvised explosives devices (IEDs) the Bureau has ever come across.

"Today's IEDs use more advanced electronics," said Special Agent Thomas Mohnal, an examiner in our Explosives Unit, based at the FBI Laboratory in Quantico, Virginia. "Our techniques and tools for dealing with these devices are also more advanced," Mohnal added, "but you still probably couldn't build a bomb much tougher to defeat than Harvey's."

Birges, Sr., said to be an inveterate gambler who had lost a substantial amount of money at Harvey's, was caught (with the help of an alert clerk at a nearby hotel who had written down the license plate of the bomb delivery van) and convicted—he never did get the ransom money. His two sons, charged as accomplices, were given suspended sentences because they cooperated with authorities. Birges died in jail in 1996.

Today, a mockup of the Harvey's bomb—built for Birges' trial—with all its booby traps and fusing mechanisms, is used for training purposes by our Laboratory Division.

Left: FEMA issued debit cards worth $2,000 in the weeks following Katrina.

KATRINA, FOUR YEARS LATER

Fraud, Corruption Cases Continue

In the devastating aftermath of Hurricane Katrina, the federal government began pouring billions of dollars into New Orleans and the Gulf Coast region to aid recovery efforts—and the criminal justice system braced for the fraud and corruption that would surely follow all that money.

Today, four years after the storm struck on August 29, 2005, the FBI and our law enforcement partners continue to aggressively investigate and prosecute Katrina-related crimes. Last Friday, for example, the United States Attorney's Office for the Eastern District of Louisiana announced 18 new felony indictments stemming from citizens fraudulently obtaining assistance from the American Red Cross and the Louisiana Road Home Program.

There have also been many cases of public corruption associated with Katrina, said David Welker, special agent in charge of our New Orleans office. "When it comes to criminal activity and public officials trying to siphon off funds meant for projects to rebuild the area," he said, "we maintain a zero tolerance policy. We won't stop pursuing these cases no matter how much time passes."

Within days of the hurricane, the Department of Justice established the Hurricane Katrina Fraud Task Force—since renamed the National Center for Disaster Fraud—to deter, investigate, and prosecute disaster-related federal crimes.

The task force—comprised of federal, state, and local law enforcement agencies, as well as the United States Attorneys' Offices—is located in Baton Rouge, Louisiana, and it has not lacked for business.

To date, more than 1,300 individuals have been indicted for Katrina-related crimes. The task force has received more than 36,000 complaints since 2005 and has referred some 22,500 to law enforcement for possible investigation. The FBI has received nearly 4,800 of those referrals.

Some of the cases are shocking. Earlier this month, a former chief of police in Lumberton, Mississippi was sentenced to 2.5 years in jail after being convicted on eight federal fraud charges in connection with lying to receive aid for a property that was not his primary residence. The former chief was found guilty of stealing government funds, lying to the Federal Emergency Management Agency (FEMA) and committing wire fraud. At sentencing, the judge ordered him to repay FEMA more than $29,000 and noted that he had betrayed the public trust and seriously tarnished the image of law enforcement.

In New Orleans, Special Agent in Charge Welker said public corruption and government fraud cases increased 243 percent during 2006-2008 compared with the years before Katrina, 2003-2005. Putting a stop to this fraud and corruption has prevented an economic loss estimated at more than $55 million, he said.

We also continue to target violent crime—the city had a high murder rate before Katrina, and it's even worse now. The New Orleans Violent Crime Task Force was established a year ago to target the "baddest of the bad," those criminals who ride the revolving door of the criminal justice system. The task force consists of federal, state, and local law enforcement officers co-located at our New Orleans office and focuses on violent crimes including kidnapping, carjacking, armed robbery, and murder.

"Katrina had such an impact on the region," Welker explained. "It turned this world upside down." When the storm hit, our headquarters in the city was ruined, and many Bureau employees there lost their homes. But now, as then, he said, "Despite the circumstances, the work of the office doesn't stop. Bureau culture is to work until the job is done—and that's just what we intend to do with Katrina crimes."

THE CASE AGAINST PFIZER

A Record $2.3 Billion Settlement

The superlatives were flying at today's press conference announcing that pharmaceutical giant Pfizer has agreed to pay $2.3 billion to resolve charges of illegal and fraudulent promotion of its products:

- The largest health care fraud settlement in Department of Justice history;
- The largest criminal fine of any kind imposed in the U.S.;
- The largest ever civil fraud settlement against a pharmaceutical company.

The case was also a massive investigation on the part of the FBI and our law enforcement colleagues, involving countless hours of work over a period of more than four years.

Speaking at the press conference this morning at Department of Justice Headquarters in Washington, D.C., Kevin Perkins, assistant director of our Criminal Investigative Division, said the record settlement "sends a clear message that the FBI and our partners will not stand by and let any manufacturer peddle their prescriptions or products for uses beyond their intended—and federal government-approved—purpose."

The case against Pfizer and its subsidiary Pharmacia & Upjohn (Pharmacia) primarily involved so-called off-brand promotion of several drugs, notably the anti-inflammatory drug Bextra. The company promoted the sale of Bextra for uses and at dosages the Food and Drug Administration (FDA) specifically declined to approve for safety reasons.

Pfizer "intended to circumvent specific FDA indications concerning their drugs by using its sales force to aggressively promote off-label uses," Perkins said. "We have interviewed numerous physicians, sales representatives, and managers who have corroborated these assertions."

Indeed, it was company employees who blew the whistle about off-label marketing—and kickbacks to physicians, who were paid to prescribe certain drugs—that first brought the case to our attention in 2005.

Special Agent Christine O'Neill, who heads the Health Care Fraud Squad in our Boston office, explained that

Kevin Perkins, assistant director of our Criminal Investigative Division, speaks to the media at the Pfizer settlement press conference.

we worked jointly on the case with investigators from the Department of Health and Human Services, the FDA, the Veteran's Administration, and the U.S. Postal Service, among others.

"These cases can be very time consuming and difficult," O'Neill said, because there are a multitude of documents to review and analyze—from sales reps' e-mail and call logs to contracts and other documents between Pfizer and physicians and health care organizations.

"When this case started," she said, "our agents were physically going through boxes and boxes of material to find evidence to support the case."

Later, we began using software that allows documents to be scanned and then searched by keyword to speed up the process. "Still," she said, "there is no getting around the exhaustive investigative work."

Criminally, Pharmacia has agreed to plead guilty to misbranding Bextra—which was pulled from the market in 2005—with the intent to defraud or mislead. The company will pay a fine of $1.195 billion and will also forfeit $105 million to the government.

On the civil side, Pfizer has agreed to pay an additional $1 billion to resolve allegations under the False Claims Act that it illegally promoted Bextra and three other drugs and paid kickbacks to health care providers.

Perkins noted that "although these types of investigations are often long and complicated, the FBI will not be deterred from continuing to ensure that pharmaceutical companies conduct business in a lawful manner." And he thanked the whistleblowers for speaking out "against a corporate giant that was blatantly violating the law and misleading the public through false marketing claims."

Left: Members of our Evidence Response Team set up their crime scene equipment after the June 10 shootings at the Holocaust Memorial Museum in D.C.

DOMESTIC TERRORISM

In the Post-9/11 Era

Nothing before or since has come close to the terror attacks of 9/11 in terms of lives lost, scope, and impact. And we know that al Qaeda led and inspired operatives still seek to strike our homeland—including with weapons of mass destruction. Which is why globally-fueled terrorism continues to occupy much of our time and attention these days.

And yet, as we were reminded by shootings in Kansas, Arkansas, and the nation's capital over just 11 days this spring, the threat of domestic terror—Americans attacking Americans based on U.S.-based extremist ideologies—is alive and well.

Today's domestic terror threats run the gamut, from hate-filled white supremacists…to highly destructive eco-terrorists…to violence-prone anti-government extremists…to radical separatist groups.

One particularly insidious concern that touches all forms of domestic extremism is the lone offender—a single individual driven to hateful attacks based on a particular set of beliefs without a larger group's knowledge or support. In some cases, these lone offenders may have tried to join a group but were kicked out for being too radical or simply left the group because they felt it wasn't extreme or violent enough. We believe most domestic attacks are carried out by lone offenders to promote their own grievances and agendas.

As with all forms of extremism, preventing homegrown attacks before they are hatched is our overriding goal. It's an especially tall order given the civil liberties we all enjoy as American citizens, including the right to free speech. Hate and anger are not crimes; neither are hard-line and poisonous ideologies. It's only when actions by groups or individuals cross the line into threats, the actual use of force or violence, or other law-breaking activities that we can investigate. That goes for lone offenders, whose high degrees of autonomy make them difficult to stop before they strike.

As a result, we're not shy about applying our full suite of anti-terror tools and capabilities to threats of homegrown terrorism. That includes our time-tested investigative techniques such as the use of surveillance and informants as well as the new intelligence skills and information-sharing channels we've cultivated since 9/11.

A few other strategies we're using:

…Our 106 Joint Terrorism Task Forces around the nation bring together our law enforcement and intelligence partners into a single team dedicated to addressing terror threats of all kinds.

…Beyond these task forces, we talk constantly with our local, state, and federal partners—those who have a finger on the pulse of their communities and can tell us about the individuals or groups on their radar.

…We're also beginning an extensive study on identified lone offenders to come up with indicators and behavior predictors that investigators can use to assess suspects.

Last year on our website, we talked about animal rights extremists and eco-terrorists and our intelligence-driven approaches to stopping them. In the coming months, we'll spotlight other homegrown terror groups to raise awareness on who they are and the threats they pose.

You can help. Be alert to potential signs of domestic terror plots and planning and contact us immediately with any information or leads.

BUILDING RELATIONSHIPS ABROAD

The View from Amman, Jordan

We opened our international office in Amman, Jordan on January 11, 2001—exactly eight months before the attack on the World Trade Centers. Today, in the post-9/11 era, our presence in Jordan and elsewhere overseas is more important than ever to our security at home.

The FBI has more than 60 international offices—called legal attachés, or legats—located around the world. Our agents who lead them act primarily as diplomats, building relationships with host countries and fostering the exchange of information with our international law enforcement partners.

"Our mission is to develop liaison relationships to further the FBI's counterterrorism, intelligence, and criminal investigations," said Special Agent Timothy Kirkham, who became the head of the Jordan Legal Attaché in June. He quickly offers a simpler explanation: "The overall goal is to prevent acts of terrorism in the United States."

Surrounded by Iraq, Saudi Arabia, Syria, and Israel, Jordan is located in a critically important region in terms of our intelligence-gathering efforts and the ongoing fight against terrorism.

"We are continually monitoring and sharing any bit of intelligence we can find," Kirkham said. "Instead of only focusing on a single bad guy, we're more focused on a region and all the pieces of intelligence from that region. We send that information back to the States to see how it fits into the overall threat picture."

"We are also facilitators," he added. "We try to meet the intelligence and law enforcement needs and requests of our host country, and we try to meet those same needs of our agents back home and our partners in the intelligence community. We serve as a conduit."

Legats can only assist in investigations overseas with the knowledge and support of the host country. That kind of cooperative arrangement requires trust, and that's where relationship building comes into play—it's a role Kirkham is uniquely qualified to play.

In addition to temporary duty assignments in Pakistan and Saudi Arabia in 2002 and 2007, Kirkham's last assignment out of our Springfield, Illinois office was as a liaison with the Arab and Muslim communities. Along the way, he learned Arabic through our Foreign Language Training Program and now speaks the language with proficiency.

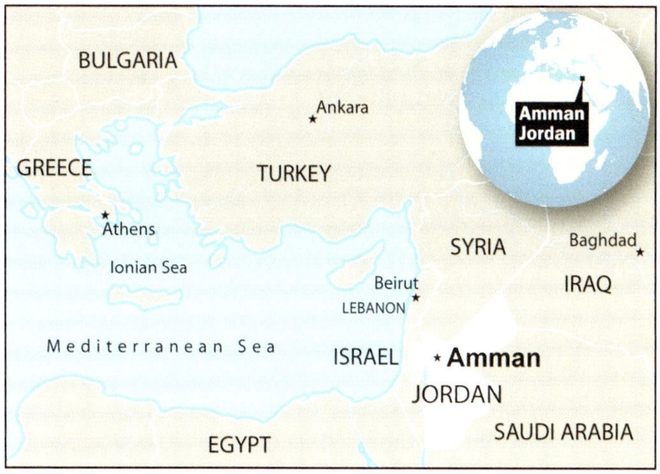

Surrounded by Iraq, Saudi Arabia, Syria, and Israel, Jordan is located in a critically important region in terms of the FBI's intelligence-gathering efforts and the ongoing fight against terrorism.

In addition, he has participated in our Arabic Language Law Enforcement Executive Development Seminar (ALLEEDS), a three-week course held annually since 2006 at the FBI's Training Division in Quantico, Virginia for Arabic law enforcement officials who don't speak English well enough to attend our National Academy program.

High-ranking Jordanian law enforcement officials have taken part in ALLEEDS, and Kirkham became friends with them before assuming his new post. "We have a different type of relationship now as a result of that experience," he said.

On a personal level, Kirkham said moving from a small Illinois town to a city with a million people has been interesting. Although he and his wife and three children live in a modern Amman neighborhood, he said, "it's common to see young boys riding donkeys, guiding herds of sheep up the hill, and the sheep stopping to graze wherever they find a patch of grass."

Of his experience with the Jordanian people, Kirkham said, "What you find out is that we're are all the same. We all want to ensure the security of our families and the security of our countries."

That, in essence, is what our legat program is all about.

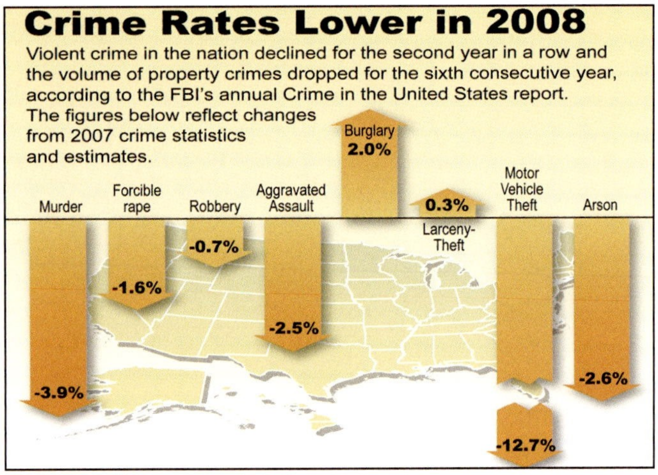

THE DECLINE OF CRIME

Even in Tough Economic Times

Unemployment, interest rates, stress—they're all on the rise as the economy is buffeted by a downturn. What's not rising, however, is crime, according to statistics compiled by the FBI that show violent crimes and property crimes declined nationwide in 2008.

The data, released today in the FBI's annual *Crime in the United States* publication, show violent crimes declined for the second straight year, down 1.9 percent in 2008 from a year earlier. Each of the four categories of violent crime offenses showed declines, including murder and nonnegligent manslaughter (down 3.9 percent); aggravated assault (down 2.5 percent); and forcible rape (down 1.6 percent).

Property crimes on the whole declined for the sixth straight year, led in large part by a 12.7 percent reduction in motor vehicle thefts. Burglaries (up 2 percent) and larceny-thefts (up .3 percent) showed small increases from a year earlier. Losses from property crimes last year are valued at more than $17 billion.

The statistics are provided to the FBI by nearly 17,800 law enforcement agencies that participate voluntarily in our Uniform Crime Reporting (UCR) Program.

Here are some of the report's estimates and findings:

- Stolen vehicles accounted for $5.6 billion in property losses in 2008, but more than half of that figure, $3.2 billion, was recovered;
- 62,807 arson offenses were reported in 2008; the average loss per offense was $16,015;
- Regionally, the South—an area that includes Maryland, Florida, and Texas—had the highest violent crime rate, while the Northeast had the lowest;
- The Western region of the U.S. had the largest year-over-year decrease in murders (down 6.8 percent), violent crimes (down 2.9 percent), property crimes (down 3.2 percent), and motor vehicle thefts (16.9 percent);
- Of the 14,180 murder victims in 2008, the age group 20-24 accounted for the most victims (2,428); and
- The estimated number of forcible rapes (89,000) in 2008 was the lowest figure in 20 years.

In addition to detailing crimes, the annual report contains data on arrests and the percentage of cases that law enforcement agencies have cleared.

Among the key findings:

- Law enforcement agencies made an estimated 14,005,615 arrests in 2008;
- The most frequent arrests in 2008 were for drug abuse violations (an estimated 1,702,537);
- Three in four arrestees in 2008 were males, and 69.2 percent of arrestees were white;
- Driving under the influence accounted for an estimated 1.4 million arrests last year;
- 45.1 percent of violent crimes and 17.4 percent of property crimes were cleared in 2008, and murder had the highest clearance rate (63.6 percent); and
- 38.2 percent of cleared arson offenses involved juveniles.

The annual report includes detailed information by law enforcement agency, location, crime type, weapon type, and demographics, among others. Please be careful not to draw conclusions of the data by making direct comparisons between cities—valid assessments are possible ONLY with careful study and analysis of the range of unique conditions affecting each local law enforcement jurisdiction.

CORRUPTION ALERT
Potential Economic Stimulus Fraud

In today's world, the most effective way for the FBI to serve the American people is to be intelligence-led and threat-driven. That means not only investigating violations of federal law after the fact, but also seeing potential threats and crimes on the horizon and being positioned to prevent them.

It's for that reason that the FBI and the Department of Justice are working now—in concert with our federal, state, and local partners, including the Inspector General community—to get out in front of possible fraud and corruption associated with the American Recovery and Reinvestment Act (ARRA).

The ARRA, signed into law earlier this year, will inject **$787 billion** into the U.S. economy, providing jobs and other resources for states and local communities. While most of those receiving the funding are honest and dedicated individuals, experience tells us that there's a good chance that some of the money could end up in the hands of a few unscrupulous government officials and others seeking to line their own pockets. A recent case in point: Hurricane Katrina.

The ARRA *does include* oversight and reporting requirements. But past investigations have shown that much of the crime is likely to occur among those who have minimal or no reporting requirements and limited oversight—that amount of money may prove too tempting for some.

The use of intelligence is key. The bulk of the funds won't be allocated until 2010 and 2011, so there hasn't been a widespread outbreak of corruption and fraud in response to the ARRA. Still, we are working now to head off potential problems by strategically collecting and analyzing intelligence to identify where we should be focusing resources.

Based on the areas that the ARRA funding is targeting, we've pinpointed specific programs that could be the most vulnerable. They include:

- **Transportation and Infrastructure:** Schemes historically involve bribery of contracting officers and inspectors and fraudulent billing for inferior materials or work not performed.

- **Education:** Funding and contracts for public schools are typically conducted by an independent board with full spending authority and little or no oversight.
- **Energy/Environment:** The increased popularity of renewable or alternative forms of energy—coupled with stimulus efforts to promote environmentally-friendly energy sources and create "green jobs"—will result in more projects and more opportunities for corruption and fraud.
- **Housing:** Funding to redevelop foreclosed or abandoned homes will be provided to state and local governments via grants, providing opportunities for public officials or grant recipients to manipulate the program for personal gain.

And when crimes like these do occur, we'll use our arsenal of lawful investigative techniques—undercover operations, court-authorized electronic surveillance, informants, etc.—that have been so effective against other types of crimes to uncover the illegal deeds.

You can help. If you suspect fraud or corruption, whether related to ARRA or another economic stimulus program, submit a tip electronically or contact your local FBI office.

Left: FBI HEAT examiners conduct forensic exams on radiologically-contaminated evidence at one of our partner laboratories. This lab is one of the national laboratories operated by the Department of Energy.

EXTREME FORENSICS

Analyzing Hazardous Materials

Last summer, eight people became sick near the reflecting pool by the U.S. Capitol in Washington, D.C. and were taken to a hospital. Later, U.S. Park Service police noticed more than a dozen dead ducks in the pool and in a nearby park. Suspecting a bio-terror attack, the Park Service contacted us, and we arranged to have samples tested. Analysis showed that the ducks were stricken with botulism Type C, which is a naturally-occurring toxin…not terrorism. And the eight hospitalized people, we later discovered, were diagnosed with an unrelated, heat-induced illness.

The FBI experts behind this fast response came from our Laboratory's Chemical, Biological, Radiological, and Nuclear Sciences Unit, or CBRNSU for short. They co-ordinated the transfer of the samples to two government labs that specialize in animals and are equipped to deal with hazardous materials.

CBRNSU was created in 2002 on the heels of the anthrax attacks the previous fall. (And the Amerithrax case has been one of its biggest investigations.) The unit's mission? To develop and maintain the FBI's ability to conduct or direct high-quality forensic exams of potentially hazardous chemical, biological, and radiological/nuclear materials and all related evidence.

"The threat facing the U.S. today is three-pronged," explains Supervisory Special Agent Margaret Eason, chief of the unit. "Chemical agents, including traditional chemical warfare agents and toxic industrial chemicals… biological agents capable of causing infectious diseases and special agriculture threats…and radiological materials or nuclear yield devices, including materials that could be used in a radioactive dispersal device or in an improvised nuclear device."

"The unit's strategy to combat these threats is also three-pronged," adds Eason.

- First, because the FBI Lab is not configured to handle hazardous materials, CBRNSU has partnered with public and private labs around the nation that can handle it and have the expertise to analyze it. As part of the agreement to partner with us, we ensure these labs follow FBI Lab standards and approved protocols.
- Second, because we still have to conduct traditional forensic exams (involving latent prints or DNA, for example) on evidence contaminated by possible hazardous materials, CBRNSU created the Hazardous Evidence Analysis Team, or HEAT. HEAT is comprised of more than 70 highly-trained forensic examiners from various FBI Lab disciplines who can be deployed as needed to our partner laboratories to perform these exams safely.
- And third, CBRNSU develops and validates methods to analyze hazardous evidence to ensure it meets legal admissibility standards. The unit has an active R&D program, working with scientific experts inside and outside the FBI.

Eason's unit is made up of highly-skilled scientists, special agents with science backgrounds (like herself), and operations specialists.

CBRNSU stays busy, often deploying members of HEAT to respond to white powder letters, suspected ricin cases, and other incidents. (Fortunately, only a small percentage of the unit's cases end up involving actual hazardous materials.) And when not physically on-site, the unit offers its expertise over the phone to FBI field offices and to our Weapons of Mass Destruction Directorate and collaborates with our Lab's Hazardous Materials Response Units. CBRNSU also provides scientific assessments for FBI and U.S. Intelligence Community products.

NEW YORK TERROR CASE
Indictment Announced

A 24-year-old Colorado resident was indicted today in a New York federal court and charged with conspiracy to use weapons of mass destruction—explosive bombs—in the United States.

Justice Department documents related to the case state that Najibullah Zazi had received "detailed bomb-making instructions in Pakistan, purchased components of improvised explosive devices, and traveled to New York City on September 10, 2009 in furtherance of his criminal plans. ... Zazi remained committed to detonating an explosive device up until the date of his arrest."

Last week, our agents arrested Zazi, a legal permanent resident of the U.S. from Afghanistan, and charged him with lying to the FBI regarding an international and domestic terrorism case. Today's indictment states that between August 1, 2008 and September 21, 2009, "Zazi knowingly and intentionally conspired with others to use one or more weapons of mass destruction."

The case is ongoing. "We are investigating a wide range of leads related to this alleged conspiracy," said Attorney General Eric Holder, "and we will continue to work around the clock to ensure that anyone involved is brought to justice." He added, "We believe any imminent threat arising from this case has been disrupted, but as always, we remind the American public to be vigilant and to report any suspicious activity to law enforcement."

The investigation is being conducted by the New York and Denver FBI Joint Terrorism Task Forces, which include investigators from more than 50 federal, state, and local law enforcement agencies.

A motion filed by the Department of Justice in New York and Colorado stated that agents learned during their investigation that Zazi allegedly conducted extensive research on the Internet regarding components of explosive devices and on "multiple occasions" purchased items necessary to produce Triacetone Triperoxide (TATP) and other explosive devices. TATP was the explosive used in the 2005 London train bombings and in the failed 2001 "shoe bomb" plot by Richard Reid.

When agents lawfully searched Zazi's laptop computer, they found bomb-making instructions and Internet searches for hydrochloric acid. While under surveillance during July and August, Zazi and others purchased unusually large quantities of hydrogen peroxide and acetone products from beauty supply stores in the Denver area—all of which can be used to make TATP.

An FBI agent outside the apartment of Najibullah Zazi in Aurora, Colorado. AP Photo.

Agents also intercepted e-mail and cell phone messages from Zazi in which he sought information about bomb-making ingredients.

The Justice Department is seeking to have Zazi transferred from Colorado to the Eastern District of New York to be arraigned on the charge in today's indictment. If convicted, he faces a potential sentence of life in prison.

Also today: In an arrest unrelated to the Zazi case but which involved the attempted use of a weapon of mass destruction, a 29-year-old Illinois man was charged in a plot to bomb the federal building in Springfield, Illinois. Michael C. Finton, also known as Talib Islam, actually tried to detonate a vehicle bomb, but he didn't realize that undercover agents made sure the bomb was inactive.

TERROR TODAY

A Report from the Director

Terrorism has been in the news a lot lately, with a series of unrelated arrests and indictments taking place across the nation—in Denver and Dallas, in New York and Springfield, Illinois—following investigations by the FBI and its partners that disrupted alleged plots to bomb a courthouse, a skyscraper, and other potential targets in our cites and communities.

Today, Director Robert Mueller testified on Capitol Hill at a Senate hearing focused on that same subject—in particular, how the threat of terrorism is being addressed eight years to the month after the attacks of 9/11. Joining him were the heads of the Department of Homeland Security and the National Counterterrorism Center—Janet Napolitano and Michael Leiter, respectively.

If you want a sense of how the post 9/11 FBI operates, then the Director's prepared statement is worth a read. It lays out the evolving terrorism threat as we see it today…as well as some of the key capabilities, initiatives, and approaches that have strengthened our anti-terror operations and turned us into an intelligence-driven organization that's more predictive and preventative.

The threat, as described by the Director, is coming at us from many different directions today:

- Credible intelligence indicates that **al Qaeda itself**—centered in the tribal areas of Pakistan and Afghanistan but also active in Europe, Africa, and elsewhere—still wishes to attack the U.S. here and abroad.
- **Other extremist groups affiliated with al Qaeda** have embraced its "vision of violent jihad" and are expanding operations, which may include launching attacks within the U.S. These groups have relocated to Pakistan and Afghanistan specifically to attack coalition troops and have coalesced in places like the Arabian Peninsula, North Africa, Somalia, Central Asia, and Iraq.
- Then there are the so-called **homegrown extremists**—inspired by al Qaeda's ideology but not connected directly to any extremist network—living and plotting attacks within our borders. The capabilities of such extremists vary widely, but in recent months we've disrupted a number of homegrown plots at various points in the planning spectrum—from scoping out targets to gathering explosives and readying to strike.
- Finally, **Americans have actually been recruited to travel overseas** to fight or train for terrorist groups. With their experience, training, and network of extremist contacts, these foreign fighters are a concern to us, both overseas and when they return to the homeland.

It takes a different kind of FBI to address these kinds of threats…and that's exactly what has been built over the past eight years.

The Bureau today is steeped in all things intelligence, as you can read in the Director's statement. We have the internal machinery in place (national collection plans, standardized roles and processes, etc.). We have the operational tools—Field Intelligence Groups in our 56 field offices gathering, sifting through, and pushing out information locally and nationally, along with more than 100 Joint Terrorism Task Forces nationwide doing the same. We have partnerships in place and working well throughout the intelligence, law enforcement, and global security communities. We are even gathering intelligence from recovered bombs and IEDs themselves. And we have an intel-driven mindset—seeing beyond single cases to the big picture threats, patiently mapping out networks of associates over months and years.

You can learn more in the Director's statement, which is posted on our website.

$80 MILLION PONZI SCAM

Even Friends Got Fooled

It sounded like a smart idea: investing in automated teller machines (ATMs) located in high-traffic retail locations around the country. The investors would recoup their money, plus an incredible 20-24 percent return, through the fees charged to the ATM customers. Seemed like a deal too good to pass up.

But investors should have done just that—because it was a fraud…a Ponzi scheme, to be more precise. The $80 million in investor funds raised over time weren't used to purchase ATMs, they were used to fuel the ruse and line the pockets of the two masterminds behind the scheme.

So says a federal indictment unsealed in the Southern District of New York last week against Vance Moore, II and Walter Netschi, charged with wire fraud and conspiracy after an investigation by the FBI.

The scam. According to the indictment, Netschi and others convincingly sold the scheme to thousands of investors—mainly small private equity/hedge fund investment companies, small businesses, retirees, and even friends. Through his front company, Netschi would "sell" individual ATMs or groups of ATMs placed in areas with a lot of foot traffic—like convenience stores, gas stations, malls, and hotels.

Netschi then allegedly had the investors sign agreements with Moore's "company" to service, process, and maintain the ATMs.

At first, investors were happy. Moore's company allegedly sent them not only monthly financial statements listing transaction histories and fees for the ATMs, but it also wired them their share of the profits. (Little did investors know that these profits were coming not from ATM fees but from subsequent investors recruited by Netschi.)

Approximately 4,000 ATMs were supposedly purchased and serviced by Netschi and Moore, but in reality—according to the indictment—about 90 percent of these machines "sold" to investors either didn't exist or were owned by other companies.

Then, the money to pay investors ran out—like it usually does in Ponzi schemes as they grow larger and larger and are unable to sustain themselves. For months, Netschi and Moore allegedly gave investors various explanations for the non-payments, blaming various banks and software glitches. They even went out and recruited more investors, said the indictment. But they couldn't raise the funds they needed, and ultimately, an unhappy investor notified authorities.

And turnabout is fair play—last week's indictment seeks $80 million in forfeiture from the alleged con artists.

How can you avoid being victimized by a Ponzi scheme? Here are a few tips:

- Be careful of any investment opportunity that makes exaggerated earnings claims.
- Exercise due diligence in selecting investments and the people with whom you invest—in other words, do your homework!
- Make sure you fully understand the investment before you hand over your money.
- Consult an unbiased third party, like an unconnected broker or licensed financial advisor, before investing.
- Don't be fooled into believing an investment is safe just because someone you know recommended it. So-called "affinity scams" are one of the favorite methods used to lure people into Ponzi schemes.

If you think you've been the victim of a Ponzi scheme or any other fraud, contact your local FBI office.

WHY PARTNERSHIPS MATTER

In Cases Like Operation Knock Out

For the past few days, Director Robert Mueller has been in Denver—the site of a recent, much-publicized terror arrest—to rub elbows with the nation's top cops at the annual International Association of Chiefs of Police conference, which showcases cutting-edge strategies and technologies and underscores the depth and breadth of law enforcement partnerships around the nation and the world.

In his keynote address today, Mueller spoke not only about the threat of terrorism, but also about crime issues that may hit closer to home for many police chiefs and sheriffs, including the continued growth of violent gangs.

"As illustrated by the recent raids in New York and here in Denver," Mueller said, "we still face significant threats to our safety from terrorists." While the primary threat continues to come from al Qaeda and those around the world who embrace its ideology, "we are also concerned with domestic terrorism, and, in particular, lone offenders."

Identifying and stopping terrorists before they act requires a level of intelligence gathering and sharing that can only result from the "continued collaboration" among law enforcement at every level, he explained. "Regardless of the threat, whether criminal or terrorist, we face the same challenges you do. We need to know where any given threat is moving, and we need to get there first."

The FBI understands that terrorism can't always be a top priority when police have to contend with violent crime in their communities, Mueller added, "but we must find a way to make the most of our shared resources to fight both crime and terrorism."

An outstanding example of sharing resources is Operation Knock Out, the nation's largest ever gang investigation and prosecution, which has been unfolding in Los Angeles. The investigation involved more than 1,400 officers from more than 40 federal, state, and local agencies. Some 200 defendants have been indicted, with more than 130 already in custody. "No one department or agency could have had this kind of impact," Mueller said. "It took a team."

Operation Knock Out targeted the Varrio Hawaiian Gardens gang and other gangs and began after the fatal shooting of a Los Angeles sheriff's deputy four years ago by a Hawaiian Gardens gang member. Last May, a 57-defendant racketeering indictment detailed the gang's war against the sheriff's department, along with its systematic efforts to rid the community of African-Americans with a campaign of shootings and violence. Raids in July were responsible for the arrests of 27 gang members.

For years, members of the investigative team met on a weekly basis and coordinated operations. One of our Los Angeles agents who worked closely on the case described the collaboration as "truly a brotherhood—each partner working shoulder to shoulder and back to back."

Mueller noted that not long ago, some in law enforcement believed they were responsible only for what happened in their own backyards. But in a global world where collecting and sharing intelligence has become critical, everyone recognizes the need for strong partnerships. "Today," he said, "we understand that we share one backyard. We are part of one team, with one mission."

OPERATION PHISH PHRY

Major Cyber Fraud Takedown

Nearly 100 people were charged today in the U.S. and Egypt as part of Operation Phish Phry, one the largest cyber fraud phishing cases to date. It's the latest action in what Director Robert Mueller described in a major address today as a "cyber arms race," where law enforcement and criminals compete to stay one step ahead of each other on the ever-expanding virtual frontier.

Cyber thieves "phish" for personal information such as usernames, passwords, and financial account details by tricking users into thinking their sensitive information is being given to trusted websites when, in fact, the sites are traps.

The defendants in Operation Phish Phry targeted U.S. banks and victimized hundreds and possibly thousands of account holders by stealing their financial information and using it to transfer about $1.5 million to bogus accounts they controlled. More than 50 individuals in California, Nevada, and North Carolina, and nearly 50 Egyptian citizens, have been charged with crimes including computer fraud, conspiracy to commit bank fraud, money laundering, and identify theft.

During the two-year investigation led by our Los Angeles office, we worked closely with the Secret Service, the Electronics Crimes Task Force in Los Angeles, state and local law enforcement, and our Egyptian counterparts—the first joint cyber investigation between Egypt and the United States. Such a cooperative effort illustrates "the power of our global partnerships," Mueller said during his speech in San Francisco to address the criminal cyber threat and what we're doing to combat it.

While Phish Phry defendants were being rounded up, Mueller told his audience, "The FBI is both a law enforcement and national security agency, which means we can and must address every angle of a cyber case. This is critical, because what may start as a criminal investigation may lead to a national security threat. … At the start of a cyber investigation, we do not know whether we are dealing with a spy, a company insider, or an organized criminal group."

In the case of Operation Phish Phry, money appears to be the driving motive. But as Mueller pointed out, "Something that looks like an ordinary phishing scam may be an attempt by a terrorist group to raise funding for an operation."

The Director delivered a major speech on cyber crime at the Commonwealth Club of California.

Mueller's remarks came during National Cybersecurity Awareness Month, an annual event sponsored by the Department of Homeland Security to help educate the public on the shared responsibility of protecting cyberspace.

"Cyber crime might not seem real until it hits you," Mueller said. "But every personal, academic, corporate, and government network plays a role in national security."

To help battle the cyber threat, the Bureau relies on strong partnerships—with law enforcement and intelligence communities worldwide, and with universities, corporations, small businesses, and citizens.

Within the government, we have established the National Cyber Investigative Joint Task Force, which brings together law enforcement, intelligence, and defense agencies to focus on high-priority cyber threats. Within the private sector we run InfraGard, where we exchange information with 32,000 partners from private industry.

But even with all our partnerships, Mueller added, "we are still outnumbered by cyber criminals." Which is why it's so important for people to do their fair share. That means protecting your home computer with firewalls, anti-virus software, and strong passwords.

"We all have a responsibility to protect the infrastructure that protects the world," Mueller said.

October 13, 2009

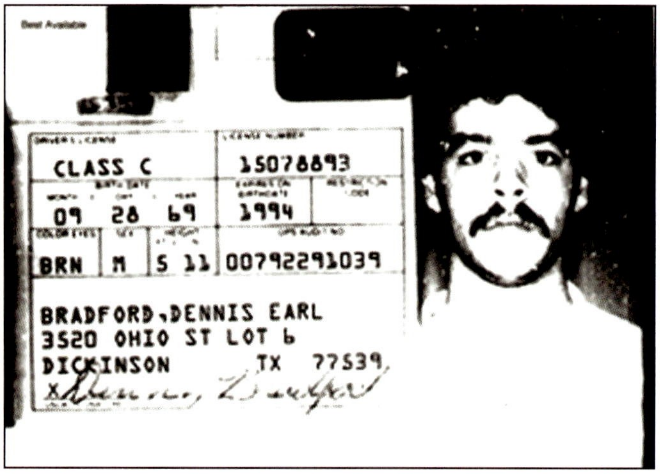

JUSTICE AT LAST

Arrest in 19-Year-Old Cold Case

On an early August morning in 1990, 8-year-old Jennifer Schuett was abducted from the bedroom of her ground-floor Texas apartment, sexually assaulted, and with her throat cut from ear to ear—unable to cry out or even speak because her vocal chords were damaged—left to die in a an overgrown field.

Miraculously, Jennifer survived. And although doctors at the time said she would never speak again, she regained her voice. Today it came through loud and clear as she thanked police and the FBI for never giving up on bringing her attacker to justice.

The arrest this morning of Dennis Earl Bradford in North Little Rock, Arkansas—the result of dedicated law enforcement officers and advanced techniques in DNA testing—marks the end of a long odyssey for Jennifer, who has made it her life's mission to speak out on behalf of victims.

"This event in my life was a tragic one," Jennifer said during a press conference in Texas, "but today, 19 years later, I stand here and want you all to know that I am OK. I am not a victim, but instead, victorious."

She thanked all those who worked on her case over the years, especially Detective Tim Cromie of the Dickinson Police Department in Texas, and Special Agent Richard Rennison, who works out of our Houston office. "They promised me that they were not going to stop until they solved the case," Jennifer said, "and they kept their promise."

Jennifer's case was pursued vigorously, but with few leads, little progress was made. In March 2008, Detective Cromie asked Rennison to take a fresh look at the case, and Rennison, in turn, asked for help from our Child Abduction Rapid Deployment Team (CARD). Eventually, evidence was sent to the FBI Laboratory for advanced DNA testing—testing that was unavailable in 1990. A DNA profile was extracted from the evidence and later matched to Bradford through our Combined DNA Index System (CODIS). His DNA was in CODIS because of a previous arrest and conviction for a similar crime in 1996.

Left: Jennifer's Schuett's description to a sketch artist of her attacker in 1990 turned out to be similar to Dennis Earl Bradford's driver's license picture from the time.

"Every bit of our success is owed to the Lab for providing us with the DNA match," Rennison said.

After her attack, Jennifer lay in a field for 12 hours before she was discovered, near death. A few days later from her hospital bed, she was scribbling notes to the police—she wrote that her attacker said his name was Dennis—and even working with a sketch artist whose drawing turned out to be amazingly similar to Bradford's driver's license picture from the time.

Jennifer Schuett

"What she did, what she went through, and to be as strong as she is today," Rennison said, "is truly incredible."

"I hope that I can be an example to others—you can have the strength to fight back," said Jennifer, who still lives near where her attack occurred. "You can get justice, no matter how long it takes."

Bradford, 40, has been charged with attempted capital murder, which can carry a life sentence. Jennifer looks forward to facing her attacker in court. "It's something I want to do," she said, "and something I have to do."

'PRETTY BOY' FALLS
The Year of the Gangster, Part 5

Two cars traveled down a country road towards the Conkle farm, two miles south of a small town named Clarkson on the eastern edge of Ohio. It was 4:10 on the afternoon of October 22, 1934, and history was about to unfold.

In one car were four Bureau agents, led by Chicago Special Agent in Charge Melvin Purvis. In the other were four local law enforcement officers, headed by East Liverpool Chief of Police Hugh McDermott.

The group was searching for Charles Arthur Floyd—known far and wide as "Pretty Boy," a nickname he hated and refused to answer to, preferring "Choc"—and they quickly realized they'd found him. Wearing a navy blue suit, Floyd jumped from a car he was riding in and bolted across a rolling field, pistol in hand.

Within minutes, Floyd would breathe his last.

Law enforcement had been closing in on Floyd over the past two days. Floyd, just 30 years old, had been in trouble with the law for about a dozen years. He'd stolen money, robbed banks, and reportedly killed some 10 people. But it was his participation in the so-called Kansas City Massacre—a brazen attack in June 1933 that killed four lawmen, including a Bureau agent—that brought the FBI into the chase.

Adam Richetti

Floyd had been traveling across the country in the fall of 1934 with another conspirator in the Kansas City attack—Adam Richetti, an ex-sheriff turned bad—and their two girlfriends when the net tightened. On the wet, foggy evening of October 20, not long after the foursome had crossed into Ohio, Floyd ran their car into a telephone poll. Floyd and Richetti camped out nearby as the women went to have the car repaired. The men were eventually spotted, and law enforcement was called.

Richetti was soon captured, but Floyd ran off on foot. Hungry and tired, the fugitive ended up on the Conkle place on the afternoon of October 22 and tried to hitch a ride. That's when the FBI and law enforcement finally caught up with him.

Charles Arthur Floyd, better known as 'Pretty Boy'

Fleeing the pursuing officers, Floyd zigzagged across the farm towards a group of trees. All eight law enforcement officers followed, calling on him to stop. As Floyd looked over his shoulder to see the pursuit, gunfire rang out. Floyd fell. "I'm done for, you've hit me twice," he said after officers approached.

As he lay dying, Floyd was questioned. He admitted his identity, but little else. He slipped into unconsciousness and died soon after.

After his death, the legend of "Pretty Boy" just continued to grow. His myth even sparked a revisionist ballad by folk singer Woodie Guthrie, suggesting Floyd saved "many a starving farmer" from losing their homes. While Floyd reportedly destroyed mortgage notes from a bank or two that he robbed in hopes of saving a few farmers from foreclosure, his reputation as a humanitarian or a "Robin Hood" is undeserved. He robbed and stole to support a lifestyle of flash and ease and didn't hesitate to shoot and kill when it suited him.

For the FBI, Floyd's death was another key victory in the war against gangsters. Next, we stepped up our search for another dangerous fugitive—Lester Gillis, aka "Baby Face Nelson." More on that story later in the next installment in our "Year of the Gangster" series.

October 19, 2009

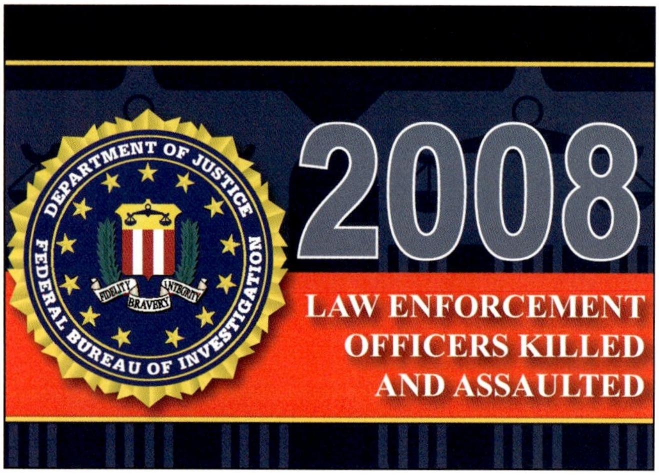

IN THE LINE OF DUTY

41 Officers Feloniously Killed in 2008

"A special agent with the FBI Pittsburgh Field Office was shot and killed at 6 a.m. on November 19 while attempting to serve an arrest warrant at a residence in Indiana Township in Pennsylvania."

The narrative describing the death last year of Special Agent Samuel Hicks is among the 41 chilling summaries of law enforcement officers feloniously killed in the line of duty in 2008. The figure, found in the *2008 Law Enforcement Officers Killed and Assaulted report*, represents a significant decline from 2007, when 58 officers were feloniously killed—indeed, it's the lowest in at least 10 years. But tempering the positive data are profiles of the circumstances that led to the deaths of 37 male and four female police officers and federal agents last year.

The annual report contains an array of data and charts on how many officers were killed and assaulted, weapons used, time of day, region of the country, even profiles of the alleged known assailants, among other things. The information, while providing a snapshot to the public of the dangers and sacrifices made by law enforcement officers, helps agencies better understand the criminal threat and tailor their training to meet it.

Here's a look at some of the data on feloniously killed officers:

- Line-of-duty deaths occurred in 19 states;
- The average age of officers feloniously killed was 39 years; the average length of service was 10 years;
- 35 were killed with firearms; 29 of them, including Special Agent Hicks, were wearing body armor when they were fatally shot;
- The average age of the alleged offenders was 32; and
- 36 of the 42 alleged offenders had prior criminal arrests.

Additionally, the report details assaults on officers and the circumstances of accidental deaths on the job each year. Here's a glance at the data:

- 58,792 officers were assaulted in the line of duty, while 26.1 percent of them sustained injuries;
- 32 percent of assaults occurred responding to domestic disturbance calls, 15 percent were during arrests; and
- Accidental deaths claimed 68 officers in 25 states, and 39 died as a result of auto accidents.

Officers who were feloniously killed represent a cross-section of the nation: men and women, black, white, and American Indian, in 19 states. They died during traffic pursuits and arrests, tactical situations, surveillance, ambushes and domestic disturbance calls. The report's victim profiles provide an important glimpse at the dangerous situations law enforcement officers face daily—a felony traffic stop in Arizona, a burglary in South Carolina, a midnight arrest in Michigan, an arrest warrant in Indiana Township, Pennslyvania.

Behind each of the report's data points are neighbors, friends, mothers and fathers who chose law enforcement ostensibly to make a difference. And in doing that they made the ultimate sacrifice in the line of duty.

In Agent Hicks' case, the Baltimore police officer-turned FBI agent was working with local police in Pennsylvania serving a warrant. A woman in the house under the influence of drugs fired a single shot, which hit Hicks in the chest above his bulletproof vest, mortally wounding him.

The raw factors in the case are reflected in the report's data. What is not is that he left behind a wife and son. At his funeral last December, FBI Director Robert S. Mueller reflected on the loss, which could be said for many of the officers killed in 2008.

"Today, we weep for Sam's family, which has lost a cherished husband, a devoted father, a loving son, brother, uncle, and grandson," Mueller said. "And we weep for our nation, which has lost one of its bravest protectors."

October 21, 2009

NEW TOP TEN FUGITIVES

List Adds Three Names in Three Days

Semion Mogilevich, a Ukrainian businessman, is charged in 40 economic crimes carried out in dozens of countries around the world, including bilking investors in a Philadelphia company out of $150 million. He is the newest addition to our Ten Most Wanted Fugitives list, and we are offering up to $100,000 for information leading directly to his arrest.

Our Ten Most Wanted Fugitives list has seen a lot of action lately, with the capture of three "Top Tenners" since July. On Monday we added **Joe Luis Saenz** to the list. And yesterday we added Mexican gang leader **Eduardo Ravelo**. The three new additions this week bring the 59-year-old list back to 10.

Since its creation in 1950, the Top Ten list has been invaluable to the Bureau, helping us capture some of the nation's most dangerous criminals. Of the 493 fugitives named to the list, 463 have been apprehended or located.

That level of success wouldn't be possible without the strong support of the public, which has helped capture 152 of the Top Ten fugitives.

Over the years, we have created several tools to help spread the word about our fugitives program, the newest of which is a "widget" that can be added to anyone's website or blog. The widget is an interactive application featuring information on all Top Ten fugitives, along with continuous feeds for FBI news and stories that are automatically updated. It's easy to add to almost any website, including Facebook and other social media networking sites, and it currently appears on more than a thousand sites around the world.

We also count on the media for help in publicizing the Top Ten list. For that reason, announcement of the three new additions to the list has been coordinated with national media.

Remember that we need your help. If you have any information about Saenz, Ravelo, Mogilevich, or any of the fugitives on our Top Ten list, please contact your local FBI office or submit a tip electronically on our website.

Joe Saenz, Eduardo Ravelo, and Semion Mogilevich are the most recent additions to the Ten Most Wanted Fugitives list, which was depleted earlier this year with the captures of three Top Tenners.

Joe Luis Saenz

In 1998, Joe Luis Saenz allegedly shot and killed two rival gang members in Los Angeles for disrespecting one of the members of his gang. Authorities believe that was just the beginning of his killing spree.

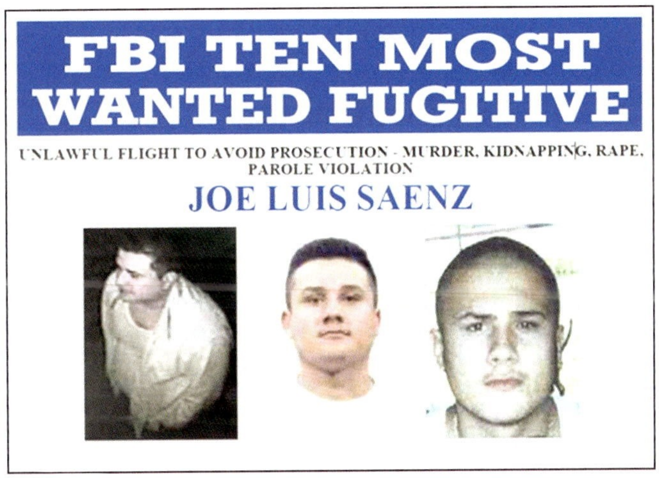

Joe Luis Saenz

According to Special Agent Scott Garriola, a 22-year veteran of the FBI who has worked fugitive cases for more than a dozen years, Saenz—the newest addition to our Ten Most Wanted Fugitives list—"is one of the worst offenders I have ever seen." Garriola added, "He's got a long career of killing, and that's just what we know about."

Less than two weeks after the gang homicides, Saenz allegedly kidnapped, raped, and murdered his girlfriend—the mother of his child—at his grandmother's home.

Saenz, now about 34 years old, is believed to be living in Mexico, working as an enforcer for a drug cartel and traveling with apparent ease across the border into the U.S. using fake identification—"legitimate I.D. fraudulently obtained," Garriola said.

We need your help. If you have any information that may be helpful to our investigation, please contact our Los Angeles office or submit a tip electronically on our website. We are offering a reward of up to $100,000 for information leading directly to the arrest of Saenz.

A few details. He is nearly six feet tall, weighs about 180 pounds, and has brown eyes and dark hair. Saenz also has a number of tattoos, although he may have had them removed with laser surgery. He goes by many aliases, including nicknames such as "Zapp," "Smiley," "Hunnicut," and "Toro."

That last name, Toro, figures in yet another murder, one that took place last year in California. In August 2008, two members of the Lott Stoner gang were stopped in Missouri by the highway patrol while driving a rental vehicle. Based on their suspicious behavior, the vehicle was searched, and troopers found $620,000 in cash in a secret panel. The money was wrapped and marked with the name "Toro." Two months later, one of those Lott Stoner gang members was murdered in his Whittier home—apparently Saenz didn't believe his story that the money was confiscated by the police.

Unbeknownst to Saenz, the victim's home surveillance system was recording at the time of the killing. "This appeared to be a cold-blooded murder," Agent Garriola said. "And judging from the videotape, Saenz seemed to be enjoying himself."

"We are hopeful that somebody will come forward in this case," Garriola said. "By his actions, Saenz has made enemies in rival gangs and even in his own gang. It would be no surprise if somebody wanted to turn him in." The agent noted that any information given to the FBI would be held in the strictest confidence.

Eduardo Ravelo

Eduardo Ravelo—leader of a violent street and prison gang operating out of Juarez, Mexico—is the second of three new additions to our Ten Most Wanted Fugitives list. We are offering up to $100,000 for information leading directly to his arrest.

Ravelo heads the Barrio Azteca gang in Juarez, and is charged with a variety of crimes, including racketeering, money laundering, and possession with intent to distribute heroin and cocaine. Although he has not been charged with murder, Ravelo and his gang members are allegedly hitmen for a Mexican drug cartel and are responsible for multiple homicides.

Eduardo Ravelo

"From everything our intelligence sources tell us," said Special Agent Samantha Mikeska, who has been working cases related to the gang since 2003, "Ravelo is a ruthless killer who has absolutely no respect for human life."

In Juarez, there is a war going on between rival drug cartels, said Mikeska, who works in our El Paso office, and Barrio Azteca is affiliated with one of them—the Vicente Carrillo Fuentes drug trafficking organization. The city, located on the other side of the border from El Paso, Texas, has had about 2,000 murders so far this year.

Barrio Azteca has approximately 600 active members who engage in murder, assault, extortion, human and drug trafficking, and other crimes. Many of the members are in U.S. and Mexican prisons and benefit from the gang's illicit profits by having funds placed in their prison commissary accounts, Mikeska said. "They are well organized," she added, "and they are dangerous."

Ravelo, also known as "Tablas," is believed to be in his mid-40s. He is 5-feet-9-inches tall and weighs between 150 and 180 pounds. He has a scar on his face and tattoos on his chest, abdomen, and back, although authorities believe he may have had plastic surgery and even altered his fingerprints. Ravelo is considered armed and extremely dangerous.

We need your help. If you have any information concerning Ravelo, please contact your local FBI office or the nearest U.S. embassy or consulate or submit a tip electronically.

"If he gets picked up," Mikeska said, "it will put a big dent in the gang's operation." The bottom line, she added: "Ravelo needs to be brought to justice."

Semion Mogilevich

A Ukrainian businessman charged with more than 40 counts of racketeering, wire fraud, mail fraud, money laundering, and other economic crimes carried out in dozens of countries around the world is the newest addition to our Ten Most Wanted Fugitives list.

Semion Mogilevich

Semion Mogilevich is wanted for his alleged participation in a multi-million dollar scheme to defraud investors in the stock of YBM Magnex International, a company he controlled—which had its world headquarters just outside Philadelphia—that was supposed to manufacture magnets but instead bilked investors out of $150 million.

As bad as that scam was, Mogilevich's continuing international criminal enterprise is believed to be much worse. "The FBI doesn't have the jurisdiction to charge him with other crimes taking place solely in other countries," said Special Agent Peter Kowenhoven, "but open-source reporting shows him to be involved in weapons trafficking, contract murders, extortion, drug trafficking, and prostitution on an international scale."

Agent Kowenhoven, who has assisted agents working this case since coming to our Philadelphia office in 1997, describes Mogilevich as a ruthless criminal. "Victims don't mean anything to him," he said. "And what makes him so dangerous is that he operates without borders. Here's a guy who managed to defraud investors out of $150 million without ever stepping foot in the Philadelphia area."

Mogilevich, who is in his early 60s, is about 5-feet-6-inches tall and weighs nearly 300 pounds. He has pockmarks on his face, may have a moustache, and is a heavy smoker. He is living in Moscow, where Russian law prohibits his extradition to the U.S.

Through his extensive international criminal network, Mogilevich controls extensive natural gas pipelines in Eastern Europe, and he uses this wealth and power to not only further his criminal enterprises but to influence governments and their economies, Kowenhoven said.

"With him, it's all about money—money and influence. And the really chilling thing is that he seems willing to work with any criminals, regardless of their ideology."

Mogilevich's money laundering network involved 27 nations around the world. At some point during our investigation, all those nations have assisted us, Kowenhoven said. "He moved money through so many countries, it made it very difficult to follow. But as a result of our investigation, we have forged great international partnerships."

Mogilevich has an economics degree and is deviously clever about manipulating funds—and investors. YBM, a public company incorporated in Canada, saw its stock price rise some 2,000 percent due to bogus financial records Mogilevich created, bribes to accountants, and lies told to Securities and Exchange Commission officials.

We are offering a reward of up to $100,000 for information leading directly to Mogilevich's arrest. If you have any information concerning the case, please contact your local FBI office or the nearest U.S. embassy or consulate or submit a tip electronically. Although Russia is his primary residence, Mogilevich has ties to the U.S. and England. He is considered armed and dangerous.

"If he's caught in any country with a U.S. extradition treaty, they could send him here," Kowenhoven said. "If Mogilevich travels outside of Russia, we're hoping someone will turn him in."

Left: A member of the El Paso Citizens' Academy takes aim during target practice. Citizens' Academy classes generally meet 10 times for three hours each session and are taught by senior managers and agents.

FBI CITIZENS' ACADEMIES

An Eye-Opening Experience

"My exposure to the FBI was very limited, just what I saw on TV," said Shannan Menya, Minneapolis.

"[The FBI] couldn't be trusted," believed Rev. Dr. Rocky Brown, Philadelphia.

"The agency was little more than interstate police," explained Azra Hussain, Phoenix.

This was what three community leaders thought they knew about the FBI **before** they completed our Citizens' Academy Program.

And **after** the program?

"I learned so many things!" says Menya.

"FBI employees are decent, down-to-earth, regular people concerned about the well-being of America and the world," says Rev. Dr. Brown.

"Its job is so much more than just policing...it's involved in so many different areas," adds Hussain.

For more than 15 years, our local Citizens' Academies have given some 10,000 community leaders an up-close and personal look at the mission and capabilities of the FBI—and changed plenty of hearts and minds along the way. Why is that so important to us? Because by building stronger partnerships with civic leaders, we are better able to do our jobs. The graduates of our Citizens' Academies enable us stay better attuned to the needs and issues of our communities, are more willing to pick up the phone and call us with information that could help solve or prevent crimes, become "ambassadors" of the FBI who dispel myths and misunderstandings about the Bureau, and often go on to join alumni chapters that work with us on all kinds of public safety initiatives.

We asked some of the graduates about their experiences...

What was your favorite part of the program?

Chuck Matthews, Phoenix: "Investigating a mock kidnapping case. We got to go out into the field and work on a simulated crime scene under the guidance of the Evidence Response Team and several agents. We collected and processed evidence...interviewed likely suspects...and after analyzing the data, determined the likely perpetrator."

Suzanne Koepplinger, Minneapolis: "Meeting my classmates—people I might not have had a chance to meet otherwise—and establishing really good relationships with them."

Sarjit Bains, Minneapolis: "Learning about some of the FBI's behind-the-scenes work, like how they provide assistance to local law enforcement agencies."

What did you learn that you didn't know before?

Dr. Saeed Fahia, Minneapolis: "The fact that you have a civil rights department that follows up on hate crimes. (Dr. Fahia noted that he grew up in Somalia, "where people had a somewhat negative view of police.")

Cathy Mick, Philadelphia: "The FBI is involved in a lot more danger than I realized. Also, they want to interact more with the public as a friend, not a foe."

Zafar Siddiqui, Minneapolis: "How the FBI handles the threats of espionage, white-collar crime, and hate crimes."

Knowing what you know now, how confident are you in the FBI's ability to protect the nation from a terrorist attack or other threats to public safety?

Jerry Fogel, Kansas City: "No doubt in my mind that except for the FBI being on duty 24/7, who knows what terrible situation we might find ourselves in...we're in good hands."

Stacy Irving, Philadelphia: "I'm more confident than ever that the FBI, working in partnership with the private sector and other law enforcement agencies, keeps our nation and our communities safe from those who wish to do us harm."

Charles Jean Baptiste, Kansas City: "I'm 100 percent confident...although we can't totally depend on the agency, the support of the community is also important."

READY TO RESPOND

Technology on Display

When the FBI is called upon to investigate a crime scene or to assist with incidents ranging from the criminal use of hazardous materials to hostage situations, we rely on the expertise of our dedicated and highly trained personnel. They, in turn, more often than not rely on technology to help them succeed in their missions. From small robots to large mobile communications vehicles, from delicate fingerprint brushes to computers capable of creating three-dimensional facial images, the Bureau has an array of sophisticated equipment and highly trained employees ready to be deployed at a moment's notice anywhere in the world.

The mission of our Evidence Response Team Unit is to carefully catalog all evidence—such as these spent bullet shells—at crime scenes. All 56 field offices have dedicated ERT components.

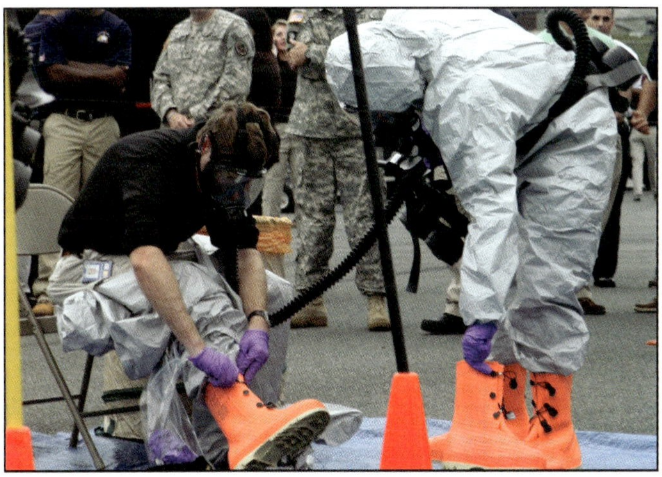

Members of our Hazardous Materials Response Team Unit illustrate a decontamination exercise. Two-man teams scrub each other's protective suits prior to removal.

Some of that technology was on display recently at our Quantico, Virginia facility, when our Science and Technology Branch hosted a demonstration featuring the response capabilities of the Laboratory, Operational Technology, and Criminal Justice Information Services divisions.

The event was designed to provide our law enforcement, public safety, and private-sector partners with an inside look at our operational capabilities.

We employ a variety of small and large robotic devices, depending on the situation. This device is radio controlled by a remote operator. Its forward pincers can be used to deliver or extract objects.

At a crime scene, examiners from the FBI Laboratory's Firearms-Toolmarks Unit, working with personnel from the Operations Projects Unit, trace bullet trajectories. Here, four trajectory lines shown in green string trace back to a single point of origin—the shooter's gun.

More pictures on the next page.

One of our many mobile command vehicles, this large unit is equipped with satellite dish communications capabilities for real-time response in emergency situations.

Our Hazardous Materials Operations Unit has a variety of response vehicles. This truck contains equipment for accessing evidence from hazardous environments, entering into confined spaces and trenches, and decontamination capability for law enforcement personnel.

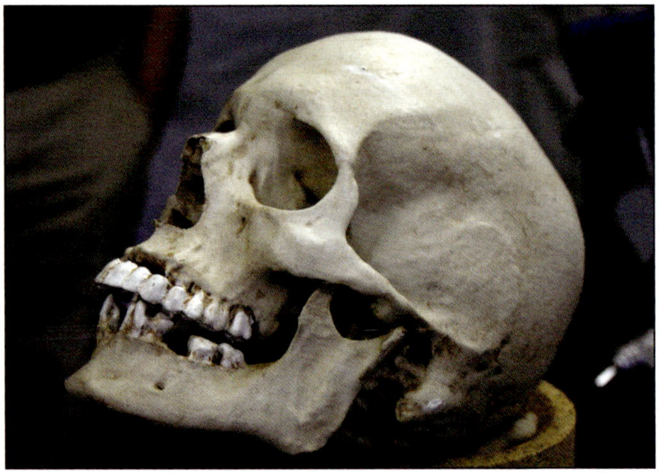

The experts in our Forensic Imaging and Operational Projects units combine talents, using laser scanning devices to make three-dimensional digital and physical reconstructed models of structures and objects such as human skulls.

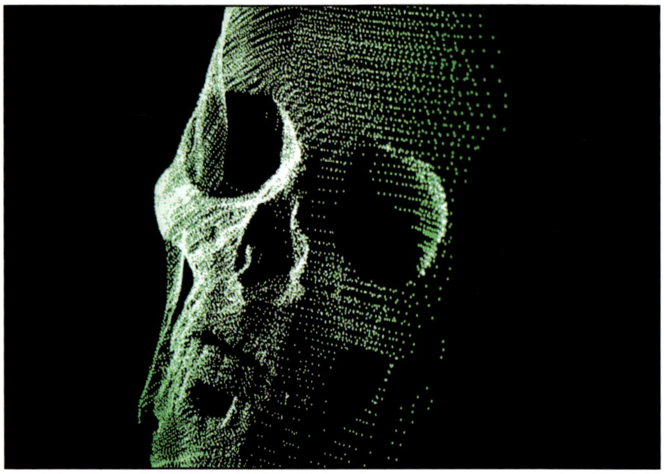

To help identify victims, sophisticated computers use digital data acquired from laser scans to create three-dimensional plastic models.

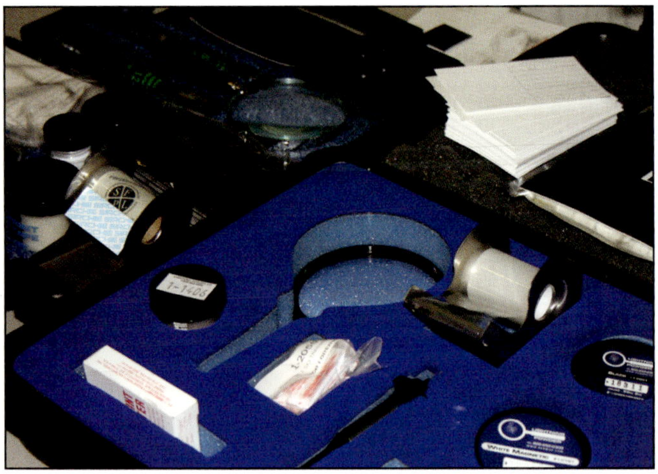

Evidence Response Teams specialize in crime scene processing, as well as evidence identification, collection, packaging and preservation, using delicate tools to glean prints from a variety of surfaces at crime scenes. Tools include dusting items, static electricity sheets, magnifying glass, tapes, and glue.

This small mock-up of a bomb was built by examiners in our Explosives Unit for the trial of John Birges, Sr., who in 1980 created what has been called an "undefeatable" explosive device. The Harvey's Casino bomb remains one of our most fascinating cases.

THE POST-9/11 FBI

Bricks and Mortar to Do the Job

You probably know that the FBI has transformed itself since 9/11 to be more proactive and preventive when it comes to terror and crime, becoming—really for the first time in its history—an intelligence-driven organization.

But that overhaul has been more sweeping than you might expect. It's had a ripple effect across the Bureau, impacting virtually every facet of our work—not just our investigations and intelligence operations, but also our recruiting, training, security, organizational structures, partnerships, records management, information technology, finances, forensics, and much more.

There's one other highly visible and important part of our operations that has undergone a similar shift: our brick and mortar facilities, particularly our 56 field office buildings across the country.

Patrick Findlay

Our field reconstruction efforts actually started following the Oklahoma City bombing but took off after 9/11 and all the changes that came with it. "We hired more agents and analysts, we established more Joint Terrorism Task Forces, we created new Field Intelligence Groups, so we simply needed more room for our people and partners and workplaces more conducive to sharing information," said Assistant Director Patrick Findlay of our Facilities and Logistics Services Division. That means large, open spaces; more Top Secret computer connectivity; and more and larger Sensitive Compartmented Information Facilities (SCIFs), where our agents and analysts often sit alongside colleagues from other agencies working highly classified matters.

Since 9/11, 16 new offices have been completed, including Houston (dedicated November 4), Jacksonville, Louisville, Omaha, and Jackson this year. Five more contracts have been awarded and are in design or construction, and 10 others have been authorized by Congress and are in acquisition. Our field office program is the largest lease-construct program in the history of the federal government. And we're planning the renovation or construction of other field offices—our goal is to make sure each one is properly sized, configured, and secured to carry out our mission.

The new Houston FBI Office was dedicated November 4. According to Director Mueller, the new building includes more room for our employees and law enforcement partners, more secure space, and stronger technology to help us meet our mission.

Working with major developers and our partners at the General Services Administration, the FBI is involved at every step of each building project. "These $40-100 million development deals are exceptionally complex and challenging," Findlay explained. "And there is a huge commitment of time and effort on the part of our field divisions—they are the ones who are on-site everyday, enabling these projects to move forward."

Findlay said we make sure the design of each building reflects the surrounding area and is environmentally friendly, following U.S. Green Building Council criteria.

FBI field offices aren't our only spaces being transformed to help us carry out our mission, though. For example:

- In 2003, our Laboratory moved out of its cramped space at FBI Headquarters and into an ultramodern facility three times as large.
- We are planning a state-of-the-art, new records facility to centrally manage all FBI records and make them available to our investigators through fast online searches.
- We're working with the State Department to ensure the effectiveness of our Legal Attaché offices in U.S. embassies overseas, building SCIFs and providing Top Secret connectivity.
- We're evaluating, relocating, or expanding all of our satellite offices (our 400+ resident agencies) around the country—46 such offices moved just last year.

In the end, said Findlay, it's all about the mission. "The better our facilities, the better we'll be able to protect our communities."

Left: Members of the Los Angeles County Sheriff's Department SWAT team demonstrate their gear and tactics to members of the CALEE program.

UNITED AGAINST MS-13

Our Central American Partnerships

The law enforcement officers from Central America and the U.S. were mid-way through a tour of the Men's Central Jail in Los Angeles when they spotted a shirtless prisoner exercising in the rooftop recreation area. The tattoos covering the man's back, neck, and head had gotten their attention—one tattoo in particular. When asked about it, the prisoner moved closer to the steel mesh barrier that separated him from the group and said the design was Mayan—"just another way to say '13.'"

Thirteen, as in MS-13, or Mara Salvatrucha. It's one of the largest and most violent street gangs in the U.S. and Central America. It was MS-13 and another trans-national gang, 18th Street, that brought this group of 27 officers together as part of a program created by our MS-13 National Gang Task Force (NGTF).

The Central American Law Enforcement Exchange, known as CALEE, is a joint FBI and State Department initiative which brings U.S. and Central American agencies together to share information and intelligence in the fight against the growing gang problem.

Because MS-13 and 18th Street cross borders to commit crimes such as murder, extortion, and drug trafficking, it's critical that law enforcement also work together across borders, sharing everything from criminal records and investigative techniques to ongoing intelligence efforts. Efficiently exchanging information as basic as types of tattoos—a person's body art often indicates his or her gang affiliation—can alert officers if new gangs or "cliques" are turning up in their areas.

"The CALEE program is fundamentally about building relationships," said Special Agent Robert Guyton, who runs the program through the NGTF. "We're talking about relationships built on personal interaction, not just by talking on the phone or sending e-mails."

The recently completed exchange program—the second of its kind—brought together representatives from El Salvador, Nicaragua, Guatemala, Costa Rica, Panama, and Belize, along with their U.S. counterparts from the Los Angeles Police Department, the Los Angeles County Sheriff's Department, and officers from Northern Virginia and several jurisdictions in North Carolina, where gang activities have been increasing. For those in the program who did not speak English, two of our Spanish-speaking language analysts provided translation.

For nearly a month, participants spent their days together in settings ranging from conference rooms and command posts to ride-alongs with officers on the street. The program started with a visit to our training facility in Quantico, Virginia and included tours of prisons in North Carolina, California, and El Salvador. At every step of the way, the Central Americans saw how U.S. agencies work—and work together—to combat gangs.

In Los Angeles, the group heard from gang experts by day and by night accompanied officers who policed the worst neighborhoods in patrol cars and even in helicopters. Along the way, many friendships were forged.

Some countries, like El Salvador, have serious gang problems. Others, like Belize, have emerging problems and are educating themselves about gang operations and tactics through CALEE. Still other countries, like Nicaragua, are learning investigative strategies and techniques to make sure their minor gang problems don't become major ones.

"The CALEE experience," said Navas Funes, of Nicaragua's Policía Nacional Civil through an interpreter, "has strengthened the ties among us and united us all in a common cause against transnational gangs."

HIGH-TECH HEIST

2,100 ATMs Worldwide Hit at Once

It was a highly sophisticated and cleverly orchestrated crime plot. And one unlike any we've ever seen before.

It culminated a year ago this month—on November 8, 2008—when a wave of thieves fanned out across the globe nearly simultaneously. With cloned or stolen debit cards in hand—and the PINs to go with them—they hit more than 2,100 money machines in at least 280 cities on three continents, in such countries as the U.S., Canada, Italy, Hong Kong, Japan, Estonia, Russia, and the Ukraine.

When it was all over—incredibly within 12 hours—the thieves walked off with a total of more than $9 million in cash. And that figure would've been more, had the targeted ATMs not been drained of all their money.

The alleged masterminds of this slick scheme—prosecutors charged earlier this month following an extensive FBI investigation assisted by other federal agencies and our partners around the globe—were three 20-something Eastern Europeans and an unnamed person called simply "Hacker 3."

Working together, the four hackers cooked up "perhaps the most sophisticated and organized computer fraud attack ever conducted," according to Acting U.S. Attorney Sally Quillian Yates of the Northern District of Georgia.

- It started when a 28-year-old Moldovan man learned of a vulnerability in the computer network of a major credit card processing company based in Atlanta. With an eye toward exploiting it, he passed that information to a hacker living in Estonia.
- The Estonian conducted "reconnaissance" on the network vulnerability and shared what he learned with a hacker in Russia.
- With the help of the three other hackers at varying times, the Russian busted into the electronic network, reverse-engineered the PIN codes from the encrypted system, and raised the limits on the amount of money that could be withdrawn from the prepaid payroll debit cards. (These cards, used by many companies, enable employees to withdrawal their salaries from an ATM.)

This individual, one of the suspected "cashers" at an ATM in the Atlanta area, is still at large. Contact our office in Atlanta at (404) 679-9000 if you have any information on him or the case.

- In addition to providing computer support, Hacker 3 managed the network of thieves around the world—called "cashers"—who used a total of 44 counterfeit cards to withdrawal the $9 million. The Estonian also managed his own cashing group.
- As the cashers went to work, the Russian took the lead in monitoring the victim company's database to track the illegal withdrawals. With the Estonian, he later deleted or tried to delete files on the computer network to cover their tracks.
- When the ATM thefts were complete, Hacker 3 —with the help of the Estonian—gathered and divvied up the proceeds. The cashers got to keep 30 to 50 percent of the money they stole; the rest went to the four hackers.

Fortunately, the company reported the breach immediately, and we quickly got to work. Our ensuing case was made with a great deal of international cooperation and even led to joint investigations overseas. Suspected cashers, for example, have also been identified and arrested in Estonia and Hong Kong.

The case is a testament to both the globalized nature of crime in today's world and the international reach of the FBI, which depends more and more on a network of 61 overseas offices worldwide to protect the U.S. from a range of national security and criminal threats.

Left: Photo courtesy of Keith Beauchamp.

WE NEED YOUR HELP

To Find Civil Rights Victims' Next of Kin

After two-and-a-half years of exhaustive investigation into more than 100 civil rights-era cold cases, the FBI has announced the next phase of our Cold Case Initiative: we're looking for the next-of-kin in 33 cases to let families know what happened to their loved ones and to possibly obtain additional investigative information.

So please look over the list on our website, and if you're a family member of one of the victims or think you may know the whereabouts of a family member, contact your local FBI office.

These cases—announced today in Baton Rouge, Louisiana by FBI Civil Rights Unit Chief Cynthia Deitle, along with cold case documentary filmmaker Keith Beauchamp—represent the last remaining investigations from our original list of 108 cold cases released in February 2007.

We've done a tremendous amount of work since February 2007, locating victims' families in 75 cases, enabling us to investigate and assess each one. "Our agents have worked tirelessly, reaching out to victims' families and interviewing witnesses, along with police officers, prosecutors, and judges," says Deitle. "They've combed through old police records, grand jury transcripts, and court transcripts to piece together a story that may have happened decades ago."

Because of our previous publicity efforts, Deitle adds, "We've also received tips and other help from the public, the media, academia, and our partners at organizations like the NAACP, the Southern Poverty Law Center, and the National Urban League."

To date, three of our 108 cases have been referred for state prosecution. In other cases, there may be no charges filed because many involve:

- Deceased suspects (47 percent of cases);
- Individuals who were already tried in state court and can't be prosecuted again in federal court because of double jeopardy;
- Deceased witnesses and old evidence that's been destroyed; or
- Deaths that weren't racially-motivated homicides (19 percent).

However, several additional cold cases have been prosecuted federally in recent years, including the 1964 murders of Henry Dee and Charles Moore. And we're pursuing leads in other cases, including the 1964 murder of Frank Morris.

Among the 36 victims whose families we're currently looking for:

- **Arthur James Hill:** shot and killed in August 1965 in Villa Rica, Georgia during an altercation with a group of white men.
- **Clarence Horatious Pickett:** beaten to death by a police officer in December 1957 in a jail in Columbus, Georgia.
- **Ann Thomas:** sexually assaulted and shot four times in the head in April 1969 in San Antonio, Texas.
- **William Lewis Moore:** a postal worker and former U.S. Marine shot and killed in April 1963 near Attalla, Alabama while marching to deliver a letter to the governor of Mississippi urging the integration of the University of Mississippi.
- **Ernest Jells:** shot to death in October 1963 in Clarksville, Mississippi by police after he allegedly pointed a rifle at officers attempting to arrest him for stealing a banana.

Once we officially close all 108 cases, we'll continue to look into racially-motivated homicides from the civil rights era that come to our attention. Protecting the rights of all Americans—whether in 1959 or 2009—remains one of our top criminal investigative priorities.

HATE CRIME

New Stats and a New Law

Hate crime has been much in the news lately, with an expansive new law put on the books just last month. Today, we're releasing our latest annual statistics on the extent of bias-fueled crime across the country, which we hope will contribute to the ongoing national dialogue and to public and private efforts to address its underlying causes.

Overall, the 2008 numbers are up slightly—7,783 incidents and 9,691 victims (including individuals, businesses, and institutions) were reported to us by our law enforcement partners across the country. But a note here: our Uniform Crime Reporting (UCR) Program doesn't report trends in hate crime stats—yearly increases or decreases often occur because the number of agencies who report to us varies from year to year.

You can find much more information in the full report, which is available on our website, broken down into categories such as locations, victims, offenders, incidents, and offenses.

Here are some of the key numbers:

- 5,542 offenses were classified as crimes against persons. Intimidation accounted for 48.8 percent of those crimes, simple assaults for 32.1 percent, and aggravated assaults for 18.5 percent. Seven murders were reported as hate crimes.
- 3,608 offenses were classified as crimes against property. The majority (82.3 percent) were acts of destruction/damage/vandalism. The remaining 17.7 percent consisted mainly of robbery, burglary, larceny-theft, motor vehicle theft, and arson.
- Of the 6,927 known offenders, 61.1 percent were white, 20.2 percent were black, and 11.0 percent were of an unknown race.
- 31.9 percent of hate crimes took place in or near homes; while 17.4 percent took place on highways, roads, alleys, or streets; 11.7 percent in schools and colleges; 6.1 percent in parking lots and garages; and 4.2 percent in churches, synagogues, or temples.

What's the impact of the new hate crime legislation on future hate crime statistics? The Matthew Shepard and James Byrd, Jr., Hate Crimes Prevention Act—the first expansion of federal civil rights laws since the mid-1990s—criminalizes violence (or attempted violence) against victims because of their race, color, religion, or

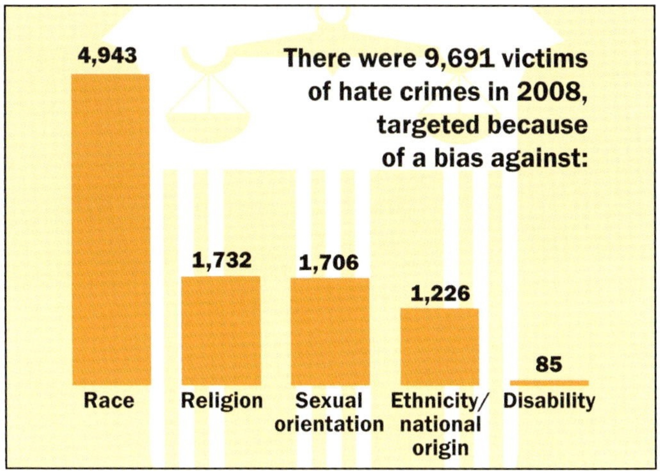

national origin, and also adds four new categories to that list of biases—actual or perceived gender, disability, sexual orientation, or gender identity. In addition, the law eliminates the provision that the crimes also be motivated by the victim's participation in one of several specific federally-protected activities.

The FBI has been collecting statistics on hate crime motivated by sexual orientation since 1991 and hate crime motivated by a disability since 1997, and we will continue to do so. In light of the new law, though, we'll begin the process of adding the collection of hate crimes motivated by gender and gender identity and incorporating them into our annual report. Our UCR staff will also work to expand their long-time training for state and local law enforcement on hate crime collection to include these two new categories of biases.

And of course, the investigation of all hate crimes that fall under federal jurisdiction—along with any assistance we can provide to our state and local partners working these cases—will continue to be a top investigative priority for us. So contact your local FBI field office if you believe you have witnessed or been victimized by a hate crime.

Left: Husayn Muhammad al-Umari (left) and Fahd Mohammed Ahmed al-Quso

MOST WANTED TERRORISTS

Two Names Added to List

Today, we are announcing the addition of two individuals to our Most Wanted Terrorists list, along with substantial rewards for information leading to their capture.

Fahd Mohammed Ahmed al-Quso is sought for his role in the October 2000 bombing of the *USS Cole* in Yemen, in which 17 American sailors were killed.

Husayn Muhammad al-Umari is wanted in connection with the 1982 bombing of Pan Am Flight 830, which resulted in the death of a teenage passenger and injury to 16 others. The flight, bound from Japan to Hawaii, carried 267 people.

The U.S. State Department's Rewards for Justice Program is offering up to $5 million for information leading directly to the apprehension or convictions of these individuals.

We are also announcing today that we have added **Abdullah al-Rimi** to our Seeking Information-War on Terrorism list. Unlike al-Quso and al-Umari, who are under indictment in the U.S., al-Rimi has not been charged but is wanted for questioning in connection with the *USS Cole* bombing.

Al-Quso, who speaks Arabic, is believed to be 35 years old. He was born in Yemen and may still be living there.

The *USS Cole* bombing took place on October 12, 2000, when suicide terrorists exploded a small boat alongside the Navy destroyer as it was refueling in the port of Aden. The blast ripped a 40-foot-wide hole in the ship. In addition to the 17 who died, many were injured.

Al-Umari, 73, who may be carrying a Lebanese passport, is one of three people indicted for the Pan Am Flight 830 bombing and is alleged to have built the device that was placed under a seat and detonated while the plane was in flight.

Sometimes called "The Bomb Man" because he is an explosives expert, al-Umari formed the terrorist group 15 May Organization in 1979. The group's mission was to promote the Palestinian cause through violence toward supporters of Israel. A Sunni Muslim who doesn't drink or gamble, al-Umari is said to enjoy smoking Cuban cigars.

Abdullah al-Rimi is wanted for questioning in connection with the *USS Cole* bombing.

We need your help to find these three individuals, all of whom should be considered armed and extremely dangerous. If you have any information concerning these alleged terrorists, please contact your local FBI office or the nearest American Embassy or consulate, or submit a tip electronically.

With today's additions, there are now 24 people on our Most Wanted Terrorists list, which was established a month after the 9/11 terror attacks. The State Department's Rewards for Justice Program, established in 1984, has paid nearly $80 million to more than 50 people who provided information that prevented international terrorist attacks or helped bring others to justice for previous crimes.

FIREFIGHT ON HIGHWAY 12

The Year of the Gangster, Part 6

A fierce gun battle had erupted just off a blacktop highway in a small and unsuspecting town called Barrington about 30 miles northwest of Chicago.

The date: November 27, 1934—75 years ago today.

On the one side were two dangerous gangsters—the hot-headed "Baby Face" Nelson and his criminal side-kick John Paul Chase.

On the other were two veteran Bureau special agents—Sam Cowley, a high-ranking inspector who was actually spearheading the hunt for Nelson, and Herman "Ed" Hollis, one of three agents who fired the shots that felled John Dillinger that summer and an important player in the pursuit of Baby Face.

In less than five minutes, what came to be known as "The Battle of Barrington" would be over. In less than 12 hours, only one of the four would still be alive to talk about it.

At the center of it all was Nelson. Ever since he'd brutally shot and killed Bureau agent Carter Baum at a Wisconsin resort that spring—and especially after Dillinger and "Pretty Boy" Floyd had fallen—Nelson had been high atop our list of public enemies. Just 25 years old—born a few months after the Bureau itself—Nelson was already a prolific and particularly violent criminal, robbing banks and reportedly murdering several lawmen and innocent bystanders along the way.

Special Agents Sam Cowley and Herman Hollis

Earlier that afternoon, agents on a stake-out had spotted Nelson, his wife Helen, and Chase driving in Wisconsin. They got the license plate and alerted Cowley. By about 3:15, after Nelson had disabled the car of another pair of agents with a hail of bullets, Cowley and Hollis caught up with the criminals at Barrington.

Lester Joseph Gillis, aka George "Baby Face" Nelson

Nelson pulled off Northwest Highway 12 (now Highway 14) at the entrance of a park and prepared to do battle. He and Chase opened fire as the agents stopped their car some 150 feet away. (Helen Gillis jumped in a nearby ditch and wasn't involved in the shooting.) The agents jumped out, took defensive positions, and began shooting. Cowley struck first—hitting Nelson with multiple rounds. But Nelson continued to fire, badly wounding the agent. Hollis bravely jumped forward and hit Baby Face in the legs with a barrage of shotgun pellets, but Nelson fired back and killed him.

Bleeding heavily, Nelson drove off with his wife and Chase. But by 8 o'clock that evening, he had succumbed to his wounds. His body was dumped in a ditch near a cemetery, most likely by Chase, and found by Bureau agents later that evening.

The Bureau had taken down a major gunslinger, but the price was high. Cowley—a steady, unassuming leader who had headed up all of the agency's major gangster cases—died early the next morning. His body was returned to Salt Lake City, his hometown, and laid in state in the Utah capitol. Hollis—another effective and ultimately heroic agent—was buried in Des Moines, Iowa.

For the young Bureau, 1934 had been a pivotal year. Working closely in every case with local and state authorities, they had taken down or helped take down Bonnie and Clyde, John Dillinger, "Pretty Boy" Floyd, Baby Face Nelson, and many of their fellow gangsters. The nation breathed a collective sigh of relief, as the gangster era passed into history. Along the way, the agency had honed its skills and put itself on the crime-fighting map, and in 1935, it had a new name to go with its growing capabilities: the Federal Bureau of Investigation—the FBI.

HOLIDAY SHOPPING ALERT

Beware of Seasonal Internet Scams

"Oh, you better watch out…" Cyber shoppers should take heed of the familiar holiday song's timeless refrain.

With holiday shopping in full swing and recession-wearied shoppers hunting for irresistibly good buys, it's a safe assumption that crooks and scammers are baiting their traps with deals too good to be true.

On Cyber Monday, the first Monday after Thanksgiving and the unofficial kick-off of the online holiday shopping season, the FBI's Internet Crime Complaint Center (IC3) issued an alert reminding shoppers to be prudent with their purse strings and personal information.

"Cyber criminals continue to aggressively create new ways to steal money and personal information," the alert states. Among the scams that prompt some 30,000 complaints each month to IC3, through its website www.ic3.gov, are:

- **Bogus online classified ads and auctions:** Criminals post products they don't have, or, in some cases, use stolen credit card numbers to purchase merchandise they offer in auctions. In another scam, criminals may promise free delivery and provide customers with free "paid" shipping labels that are fake and won't be honored by shippers. **Tips:** Don't provide financial information directly to sellers—use a legitimate payment service. Check each seller's feedback ratings and proven track record.
- **Phony gift cards:** As with merchandise, be cautious about buying gift cards through classifieds or auctions. **Tip:** Buy directly from a merchant or authorized retailer. Counterfeit cards won't be honored.
- **Phishing:** These time-tested scams arrive by e-mail or text message, directing recipients to follow a link or call a number to correct or update account information. Would-be victims are sent to fraudulent or spoofed websites that look legitimate and told to provide their account information and personal details. **Tips:** Don't respond to unsolicited e-mail. Don't click on e-mail links or download attachments from unknown senders.

The leading retail association predicted 96 million Americans would shop online on Cyber Monday alone, and millions more during the month of December. For criminals, the numbers spell opportunity. Shoppers, meanwhile, should exercise the same caution they would in a crowded mall—eyes wide open, protecting themselves and their money.

"If you're shopping online, make sure the website is secure and it's not a cloned website," says Supervisory Special Agent Leslie Hoppey, acting unit chief of the Internet Crime Complaint Center. "If you want to deal with a business, go directly to their official website."

IC3 last year received more than 275,000 complaints and reported losses of $265 million—an average of $931 per complaint. The most common complaints in 2008 were non-delivered merchandise or payment (32 percent) and auction fraud (25 percent).

Agent Hoppey offers some additional tips—have the latest version of security software installed on your computer and make sure online transactions are secure. And she offers a holiday classic as time-honored as re-gifting: "If it looks too good to be true, it probably is."

'FBI, THIS WEEK' AT 1,000

On Your Radio (and iPod, Too)

Fascinating investigations of mobsters, terrorists, spies, and serial killers. Emerging scams. Fugitives on the run and computer viruses on the loose. Major crime-fighting innovations. Memorable moments in FBI history.

If you're interested in all things FBI—as told straight by our case agents, senior execs, scientists, and other experts—then check out our long-running radio program, "FBI, This Week."

This program airs every Friday on ABC Radio and various talk shows and stations across the country. If you're not a radio regular, not to worry—you can also download it from iTunes or catch it on this website.

The show first hit the airwaves back on September 21, 1990, tackling a hot topic of the day—the savings and loan crisis. With today's episode—which, by the way, talks about a hot topic of *our* day, cyber crime—the program celebrates a remarkable milestone of its own: its 1,000th episode.

Looking back, the long list of shows reads like a walk through FBI history, a snapshot of Bureau successes and news over nearly 20 years.

"The purpose of 'FBI, This Week' has always been to provide a window into the Bureau—to let people know what we're up to and how it impacts their daily lives," explains Neal Schiff, the veteran FBI newscaster who has produced and narrated each episode. "The fact that the program has lasted two decades proves that people care about what we're doing to protect them and want to know about crime and security issues that impact their communities."

Schiff gets particular satisfaction from featuring top ten fugitives and wanted child molesters. "We need to pull out the stops to find these people," he says. He cites the case of mobster James "Whitey" Bulger—last year, audio clips of Bulger were played on back-to-back episodes of the show. "Faces change over time, but a person's voice is very distinct, so it was great to get that on the air."

The Bureau has had its own radio programs for more than four decades—starting with "FBI Washington," which aired from 1965 to 1990. That show was first hosted by Fred Foy, the announcer for "The Lone Ranger" radio program, and then by ABC television booth announcer and former radio actor George Ansbro, who retired in 1990.

Neal Schiff producing the show in his office at FBI Headquarters.

Today, Schiff produces three more radio programs and podcasts:

- "Gotcha," which since the late 1990s has highlighted our closed cases;
- "Inside the FBI," our first podcast, launched last October; and
- "Wanted by the FBI," a second podcast that grew out of discussions with fugitive publicity coordinators as another way to enlist the public's help in finding missing kids, fugitives, bank robbers, and more.

For Schiff, the first 19 years of "FBI, This Week" have passed quickly. "It hardly seems like a thousand episodes," he says. "The length and breadth of the FBI's work—and its impact on just about everyone—has always given me plenty of interesting cases and breaking news to talk about."

Yes, and please stayed tuned to your radio dial: there are plenty more shows to come.

Left: The attack on Pearl Harbor. Photo courtesy of the National Archives. Inset: Special Agent in Charge Robert L. Shivers

PEARL HARBOR LEGACY

Remembering Robert Shivers

It was 68 years ago this morning—December 7, 1941—that a torrent of bombs fell on Pearl Harbor, a stealth attack that took the lives of more than 2,400 Americans and thrust the nation headlong into its second major war of the century. It was a day—filled with sacrifices and heroism—that will never be forgotten.

The contributions of one man who made a major impact in the aftermath of the attack should also not be forgotten. His name is Robert L. Shivers, and he was the special agent in charge of our office in Honolulu on that fateful day.

Shivers had been handpicked by Director J. Edgar Hoover to run the Honolulu office precisely because of his leadership skills. Smart and genteel, Shivers was minted as a special agent in 1920. After serving across the South and Midwest and in New York, the Tennessee native was tapped to lead field offices in Pittsburgh, Buffalo, and Miami. But because of nagging health issues, he went on restricted duty in the late 1930s.

In the summer of 1939, however, Europe was on the verge of war, and with the U.S. supporting the Allied cause, the FBI was plenty busy trying to prevent espionage and sabotage at home. In August, Hoover turned to Shivers to re-open the now strategically important FBI division in Honolulu.

Shivers got to work. Within a few months, he developed strong relationships with local police as well as with Army and Navy forces, and he also began making contacts in the islands' Japanese communities. These deepened when he and his wife began caring for a Japanese schoolgirl named Shizue Kobatake (later Suzanne or Sue). Despite the differences in their backgrounds, they became like a family.

Then came December 7. Within minutes of the attack, Shivers alerted Director Hoover, who quickly put the Bureau's contingency war plans into effect.

For his part, Shivers—who had already made progress in sorting out the FBI's division of intelligence and security responsibilities with the Navy—immediately placed the Japanese Consulate under police guard, both to protect the diplomats from retaliation and to prevent their escape. His agents seized a large quantity of suspiciously coded documents that consulate employees tried to hastily burn and began running down key cases of espionage (especially that of Otto Kuehn).

Another major issue involved the 150,000 people of Japanese ancestry in Hawaii—roughly a third of the population. Some argued that they should be taken into custody. Shivers and key members of the armed services and territorial government strongly disagreed and made a vital difference in preventing the kind of mass internment that happened on the mainland (which Director Hoover opposed, but that's another story). Only a few thousand Japanese nationals considered a security risk ended up being detained.

Shivers soon gained respect across the island, earning significant authority from its military governor. His only critic was a local U.S. Attorney, who thought he dealt with the Japanese on the islands "too leniently."

History has taken a different view—and so did Shivers' contemporaries. When his health forced him to retire in 1944, Shivers was lauded by the territorial Senate of Hawaii both for "safeguarding Hawaii's internal security" and for displaying "sympathy, sound judgment, and firmness."

PLAYING WITH FIRE

The Dangers of Improvised Explosives

It was late on a recent Friday night when local authorities responded to a residential explosion. They found a middle-age man with serious injuries to his left hand and face—and they also found chemicals, fuses, and empty rifle shells in the home. The man later told our agents that out of boredom he was trying to make an explosive device from a "recipe" he found on the Internet.

As bizarre as the story might seem, our experts say that people experimenting with improvised (homemade) explosives is an all-too-common occurrence.

"Probably once a month I hear from law enforcement somewhere about someone blowing their hand off while experimenting in this manner," said Kirk Yeager, an examiner in our Explosives Unit at the FBI Laboratory who is recognized as one of the foremost experts in the area of improvised explosives.

Yeager, a Ph.D chemist who joined the Bureau about 10 years ago, created the National Improvised Explosives Familiarization Initiative (NIEF) in 2007 to address the growing concern about terrorists—and others—who mix common household materials and over-the-counter products to make dangerous explosives.

NIEF is operated as a joint partnership with our Weapons of Mass Destruction Directorate, the Critical Incident Response Group, and the FBI Laboratory. Initially, 250 of our special agent bomb technicians and weapons of mass destruction coordinators received training about the kinds of products—ones typically found under kitchen sinks and in garages—that can burn or explode when combined and how to disrupt or dismantle devices that use such products.

Then the training expanded to include regional bomb techs, members of our Joint Terrorism Task Forces, and other first responders. So far we've trained nearly 400 people in 11 regions nationwide. And many of them will bring the NIEF training to others in their communities, including parents and children.

Those who experiment with improvised explosives, Yeager said, may be bright youngsters curious about things that explode, those who actually want to cause destruction, or "perennial adolescents who just like to see things blow up."

The three-day NIEF training culminated with the detonation of a 25-pound improvised explosive inside a car's passenger compartment. The explosion destroyed the vehicle.

The Internet has certainly added to the problem. Not only do online searches yield recipes for making powerful bombs, they provide access to videos that offer step-by-step instructions.

"One of our best weapons to deal with this issue is public awareness," said Donald Sachtleben, a retired special agent who leads many of the three-day NIEF training sessions. During the last day of training at our Quantico, Virginia facility earlier this month, members of regional bomb squads prepared some of the compounds they had learned about in the classroom for a live-fire demonstration. Later, they heard the deafening boom and felt the shock wave from 700 yards away when a mere 25 pounds of explosive material—small enough to sit unnoticed in the back seat of a car—split a two-ton vehicle in half, pulverizing everything but the engine block.

"We are all fascinated by bright lights and loud sounds," Yeager said. "It's something almost primal." But most people have enough sense to keep from experimenting with improvised explosives. Those who don't have enough sense—whether out of boredom or curiosity—should realize they are risking their own lives as well as others', Yeager added. "At the end of the day, they are making things just as dangerous as the most determined terrorist."

THE PATH TO TERROR

The Jihadists of Georgia, Part 1

They were a couple of young Americans with terror on their minds, two middle-class kids barely out of high school who lived seemingly normal lives in and around Atlanta while secretly taking up the mantle of violent jihad, who in the span of a year went from being extremist wannabes to trusted brothers of terrorist operatives across the globe.

Now, following their convictions in federal court earlier this year and sentencings this week, they are each headed to prison for quite some time.

Their names are Ehsanul Islam Sadequee and Syed Haris Ahmed, and their story is indicative of both the evolving homegrown extremist threat and the FBI's post 9/11 intelligence-driven investigations.

When Sadequee and Ahmed met at a midtown Atlanta mosque, neither was yet 21. Ahmed, who was born in Pakistan and moved to this country at about age 12, was a mechanical engineering student at Georgia Tech. Sadequee, a Bangladeshi-American born in Virginia, was working at an Atlanta non-profit while living at home with his mother and siblings in the suburb of Roswell.

The two soon became friends, finding that they shared a similar interest: violent jihad. They started spending hours online—chatting with each other, watching terrorist recruitment videos, and meeting like-minded extremists.

But they clearly wanted to do more than just stand on the sidelines. Fueled by their growing connections in cyberspace, Sadequee and Ahmed made a series of journeys that drew them further and further into a web of terror.

- In late 2004, they traveled to rural northwest Georgia, shooting paintball guns and practicing attack techniques as part of basic paramilitary training.
- The following March, they hopped on a Greyhound bus to Canada, where they spent a week talking terror with three jihadists they met on the Internet. One was an alleged member of the "Toronto 18," a terror cell that later plotted to bomb the Canadian Parliament and other targets before being exposed in 2006.
- In April 2005, Ahmed and Sadequee drove a pickup truck to the nation's capital and cased a series of landmarks—including the U.S. Capitol and the Pentagon—making more than 60 short video clips to help establish their extremist credentials. Sadequee sent several clips to Younis Tsouli—aka "Irhabi007" ("Terrorist 007" in Arabic), an al Qaeda webmaster, recruiter, and propagandist—and to Aabid Hussein Khan, a facilitator for two Pakistan-based terrorist groups. Both Tsouli and Khan have since been convicted of terror offenses in the U.K.
- That summer, Ahmed and Sadequee took separate trips overseas. Ahmed went to Pakistan, meeting with Khan and asking to attend a training camp and engage in jihad (he was talked out of it by his family). Sadequee was off to Bangladesh, where he joined with Tsouli and a Swedish extremist named Mirsad Bektasevic to form a violent jihadist organization known as "Al Qaeda in Northern Europe." In October, just a few days after being in contact with Sadequee, Bektasevic was arrested in Sarajevo armed to the teeth; he was later convicted of terrorism.

What Sadequee and Ahmed didn't know was that for some time, they were being tracked by the FBI and its partners. In part two of our story, we'll talk about how our investigation unfolded.

INTEL AT WORK
The Jihadists of Georgia, Part 2

It was a tip from a foreign intelligence partner that set the case in motion.

In the summer of 2005, we learned that a central player in a terrorism investigation in another country was in e-mail contact with someone in the Atlanta area.

With appropriate court orders, our Joint Terrorism Task Force in Atlanta quickly tracked down who that person was. It was a 19-year-old American named Ehsanul Sadequee, who was also exchanging regular e-mails, we discovered, with a 20-year-old Georgia Tech student named Syed Haris Ahmed.

Initially, our investigation—code-named "Northern Exposure"—was focused on finding out what the two young men were up to and why Sadequee was trading e-mails with a terrorism suspect. We began both electronic and physical surveillance on each one and began tracking their financial and travel patterns with the help of partner agencies in the U.S.

We soon uncovered two key facts. One, both Sadequee and Ahmed were in touch with terrorist suspects in nearly a dozen nations around the world. And two, a great deal of this contact was via the Internet.

With our new post-9/11 intelligence-driven mindset, the last thing we wanted to do at that point was to rush in and make arrests. It was far more important to tease out information on all the players who might be connected to Sadequee and Ahmed, to paint a larger picture of this online and offline network of extremists, and to share that information with our national and international colleagues.

As discussed in part one of our story, our investigation revealed that Sadequee and Ahmed ended up casing U.S. targets, supporting and sharing information with terrorists around the globe, and traveling overseas to act on their desire to wage violent jihad. Some of our intelligence came from our overseas partners, who discovered links from their terrorism suspects to Sadequee and Ahmed. And the FBI shared its intelligence on terror suspects uncovered during our investigation of the two Atlanta extremists.

In March 2006, we approached Ahmed to see if he would cooperate in the case. Though he tried to deny his illegal activities, Ahmed made incriminating statements and secretly contacted Sadequee to warn him of our investigation. We arrested Ahmed soon after, and Sadequee was arrested in Bangladesh the following month. Both were convicted in separate trials this year, and sentenced on December 14.

Mark Giuliano, former assistant special agent in charge of our Atlanta office and current head of the FBI's Domestic Terrorism Strategic Operations Section, played a key role in the investigation.

A satisfying end to the case, but this investigation had a far broader and more significant outcome: thanks to unprecedented global cooperation, governments in nearly a dozen nations have arrested more than 40 individuals and disrupted an untold number of terror plots.

"Sadequee and Ahmed never pulled a trigger or set off a bomb, but they were making plans and working with known terrorists worldwide," says Atlanta Special Agent in Charge Gregory Jones. "By using an intel-driven approach, we not only stopped these guys from doing harm, we took out a larger web of extremists."

In the end, a network of terrorists was brought down by another network: a determined group of law enforcement and intelligence agencies from around the world working in unison to share information, compare evidence, and disrupt terrorist plots.

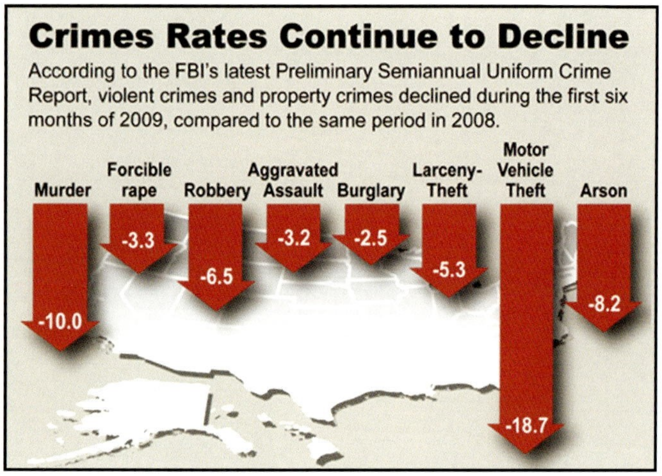

CRIME RATES FALL

In the First Half of 2009

For the third year in a row, our *Preliminary Semiannual Uniform Crime Report* shows that violent crime, property crime, and arson have decreased. The latest report compares January-June 2009 figures with the same time period in 2008.

Crimes reported to our Uniform Crime Program are down collectively: violent crime overall decreased 4.4 percent, property crime 6.1 percent, and arson 8.2 percent.

Individual crimes are also decreasing across the board:

- Murder (down 10.0 percent);
- Forcible rape (down 3.3 percent);
- Robbery (down 6.5 percent);
- Aggravated assault (down 3.2 percent);
- Burglary (down 2.5 percent);
- Larceny-theft (down 5.3 percent); and
- Motor vehicle theft (down 18.7 percent).

Other interesting highlights:

- Murder was lower in all four regions of the country, with the largest decreases in the Northeast (13.7 percent) and the West (13.3 percent).
- Motor vehicle thefts decreased significantly in all four regions of the country (Northeast, 19.3 percent; Midwest, 21.4 percent; South, 17.8 percent; and West, 18.2 percent).
- While violent crime and aggravated assault were down in cities of more than one million people (7.0 percent and 6.2 percent, respectively), in cities of populations between 10,000 and 24,999, violent crime rose 1.7 percent and aggravated assault rose 3.8 percent.
- While both metropolitan areas and non-metropolitan areas experienced decreases in violent crime and property crime in general, non-metropolitan counties saw increases in robbery (3.8 percent) and arson (1.2 percent).
- On a regional basis, the only uptick in any crime was a slight increase in burglaries in the South (up 0.7 percent).

Developing this national view of crime is a collective effort of the FBI and the thousands of city, university/college, county, state, tribal, and federal law enforcement agencies that submit the data to us. Participating agencies throughout the country voluntarily provide reports on crimes known to police and on persons arrested.

The data has become a source of information used widely by police administrators, government policy makers, social science researchers, the media, and others concerned about the impact of crime in our communities. We do, however, caution against drawing conclusions from our data by making direct comparisons between law enforcement agencies—valid assessments are possible ONLY with careful study and analysis of the range of unique conditions affecting each local law enforcement jurisdiction.

The FBI has been collecting crime data from our law enforcement partners since the 1930s. Over the years, the scope of the program has expanded in response to suggestions from law enforcement advisory groups or to comply with federal mandates. Today, the culmination of this national data collection is three annual publications: *Crime in the United States*, *Hate Crime Statistics*, and *Law Enforcement Officers Killed and Assaulted*, as well as semiannual reports like this one.

The full 2009 *Crime in the U.S.* report will be released later next year.

MICHAEL JACKSON

Investigative Files Released

In response to Freedom of Information Act requests, the Bureau has released its investigative files on the late entertainer Michael Jackson, who died earlier this year.

The records total 333 pages, divided into seven files. They detail the FBI's investigation of a man who threatened to kill Jackson, as well as various forms of assistance to California authorities in two cases involving allegations that Jackson had abused children. It should be emphasized that none of these allegations were ever proven in court.

The files are available on the Freedom of Information Act/Privacy website, but here is a quick rundown of what they contain.

The **first file**—9A-LA-142276—was opened by the Los Angeles FBI office when it was asked to lead a federal case against a California man already under arrest for sending numerous threatening letters. The man—who falsely claimed to be the son of mobster John Gotti—had staked out Jackson's house and threatened to kill him, the U.S. president, and others. He was ruled incompetent to stand trial and sent to prison for two years.

The **second and third files**—62D-LA-162715 and 62D-LO-11779—involve the Bureau's support of local law enforcement. In 1993, the Los Angeles and the Santa Barbara Police departments formed a task force to investigate an allegation that Jackson had molested a young boy. FBI field divisions in Los Angeles and New York—as well as Bureau overseas offices in Manila and London—provided assistance in that case. Investigators gathered public records on Jackson, interviewed a potential witness, and followed various other leads. The FBI assisted Los Angeles Police Department detectives who traveled to the Philippines to interview possible witnesses and shared news reports from London about a potential victim. The U.S. Attorney declined to pursue a federal investigation, including a possible violation of the Mann Act (transporting a minor across state lines for immoral purposes), and no charges were filed by the state.

The **fourth file**—95A-HQ-1148159—concerns a 1995 request by a U.S. Customs agent in Florida that the Bureau examine a VHS videotape connected with Jackson to see if it contained child pornography. Forensic specialists discovered that the tape was a "poor quality

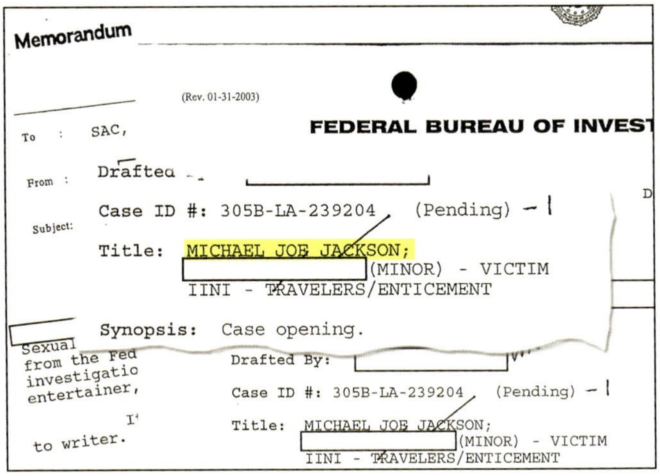
Memorandum

(Rev. 01-31-2003)

FEDERAL BUREAU OF INVEST

To : SAC,

From : Drafted

Subject: Case ID #: 305B-LA-239204 (Pending)

Title: MICHAEL JOE JACKSON; (MINOR) - VICTIM
IINI - TRAVELERS/ENTICEMENT

Synopsis: Case opening.

Drafted By:

Case ID #: 305B-LA-239204 (Pending)

Title: MICHAEL JOE JACKSON; (MINOR) - VICTIM
IINI - TRAVELERS/ENTICEMENT

third or fourth generation recording" and informed the Customs Service of their findings.

In 2003, Jackson was charged by the state of California with molestation and other counts. The **final three files**—62D-LA-236081, 252B-IR-6808, and 305B-LA-239205—detail the Bureau's support to local law enforcement during the ensuing investigation. The first of these files describes an FBI response to a Los Angeles Police Department request to analyze computers and digital media obtained from Jackson's home under court warrant. The second involves a request by the Santa Barbara County District Attorney for help and guidance from behavioral analysts in the FBI's Critical Incident Response Group. In the last of the three files, an FBI agent from Los Angeles traveled to New York to interview a potential witness. The agent found this individual unwilling to cooperate and closed the matter. The case went to court in 2005, and Jackson was acquitted of all charges.

CAN YOU CRACK A CODE?

Try Your Hand at Cryptanalysis

We've challenged you before—in November 2007, December 2008, and May 2009—to unravel a code and reveal its secret message like the "cryptanalysts" in our FBI Laboratory.

In our latest quiz, we've switched gears a bit, using pictogram symbols based on Native American motifs. And with more than 50 words to decipher, it's our longest one so far.

For the first time, we're also posting the answer (see the bottom of this page) in case you are stumped. We ask, however, that you not post the solution on the web so that everyone can have a chance to give it a try.

Once again: If you want a primer on basic cipher systems and how to break them, see our article "Analysis of Criminal Codes and Ciphers." And if you're a youngster, we suggest you start with the code on our Kids' page.

Good luck!

Note: Sorry, but cracking this code doesn't guarantee you a job with the FBI! But do check our careers at FBIJobs.gov.

The answer to the cryptographic is as follows:

This is our hardest quiz so far. It is longer, of course, with more than twice as many words as our last cryptographic challenge. It also features a new set of pictogram symbols based on Native American symbols and motifs for each character of the alphabet. Thanks for participating, and kudos on cracking the code.

THE YEAR IN REVIEW
A Look at FBI Cases, Part 1

Terrorists bent on murder and destruction. Elected officials on the take. Cyber crooks hacking networks and emptying bank accounts. Fraudsters using scams old and new to pilfer billions of dollars from unsuspecting Americans.

The FBI worked thousands of investigations during 2009—from art crime to weapons of mass destruction violations, often in close concert with our partners. As the year comes to a close, here is a rundown of some of the Bureau's most significant cases.

In this first segment, we'll focus on our top investigative priority: protecting the nation from terrorist attack. The threat posed by extremists is real—and it continues to morph and evolve in new and dangerous ways, like most recently, the Christmas Day incident. Working with a range of local, state, federal, and international partners, we headed off a number of potential plots on U.S. soil.

Here are some of the top terror cases of 2009, in reverse chronological order:

Georgia jihadists: With little more than an Internet connection and the radicalizing influences of overseas terrorists, two middle-class young men in Atlanta went from rhetoric to plotting jihad and were sentenced earlier this month.

David Coleman Headley: The U.S. citizen was arrested in October for planning terrorist attacks against a Danish newspaper and two of its employees. New charges this month in this ongoing case allege he took part in the conspiracy surrounding the 2008 Mumbai attacks.

Somalia: In February, the FBI reported that young men from Minneapolis were traveling to Somalia to join extremists fighting for control of the country. One of those men became who was believed to be the first U.S. citizen to carry out a terrorist suicide bombing after launching an attack in Somalia. By November, 14 defendants were charged with recruiting people from the U.S. to train or fight on behalf of extremist groups in Somalia.

Najibullah Zazi: The 24-year-old Colorado resident was arrested in September, along with his father and another man, for conspiracy to use weapons of mass destruction against U.S. citizens. Zazi traveled to New York City on September 10, 2009 "in furtherance of his criminal plans," according to the Department of Justice.

Attempted bombing of federal building: In September, a U.S. citizen was arrested in connection with a plot to detonate a vehicle bomb at the federal building in Springfield, Illinois.

Attempted skyscraper bombing: Also in September, a 19-year-old Jordanian citizen who espoused violent jihad was arrested for attempting to blow up a 60-story glass office tower in Dallas, Texas.

North Carolina takedown: In July, seven men, including a father and two sons, were charged with conspiring to provide material support to terrorists and to wage jihad overseas. The heavily armed group trained in the U.S., raised money to support their training, and recruited and radicalized others.

Synagogue plot: In May, four people were arrested outside a New York synagogue and charged with planning to blow up Jewish targets and shoot down military planes.

Liberty City Six: In May, a Miami jury convicted five men of providing material support to al Qaeda and planning attacks on U.S. targets, including the Sears Tower in Chicago.

Ali al-Marri: In May, the al Qaeda "sleeper" operative working in the U.S. pled guilty to charges relating to his role in the 9/11 attacks.

THE YEAR IN REVIEW

A Look at FBI Cases, Part 2

Together with our partners in the law enforcement and intelligence communities, the FBI worked thousands of investigations during 2009, everything from cyber crime and espionage to public corruption and billion-dollar fraud schemes. As the year draws to a close, we thought readers would be interested in a look back at some of 2009's most significant cases.

Part 1 focused on terrorism cases. This segment highlights some of the year's top cases from the FBI's other investigative priorities:

Espionage: In November, a former State Department official and his wife pled guilty to a 30-year conspiracy to provide classified military information to Cuba. (Preventing and exposing intelligence activities—spying—on U.S. soil remains one of the Bureau's top investigative priorities because it strikes at the heart of national security.)

Cyber heist: Also in November, four hackers were charged with masterminding the simultaneous theft of $9 million from 2,100 ATMs from around the world. They did it all in 12 hours, illustrating the global reach—and threat—of cyber crime. (The arrests illustrated the importance of global law enforcement partnerships.)

Public corruption: In August, former Louisiana Congressman William J. Jefferson was convicted of bribery, racketeering, and money laundering. In November, a federal judge sentenced the 62-year-old to 13 years in prison and ordered him to forfeit more than $470,000.

Operation Phish Phry: Nearly 100 people were charged in the U.S. and Egypt in October in one the largest cyber fraud phishing cases to date. The defendants targeted U.S. banks and victimized hundreds and possibly thousands of account holders by stealing their financial information and using it to transfer money to bogus accounts.

Operation Cross Country: As part of the FBI's Innocence Lost National Initiative, 100 children victimized through prostitution were recovered in two separate multi-city sweeps. More than 1,200 individuals—including 60 pimps—were arrested on state and local charges.

Operation Knock Out: The nation's largest gang investigation and prosecution underscored the growing gang problem in the U.S. and the negative impact gangs have on communities. The Los Angeles investigation involved more than 1,400 officers from more than 40 federal, state, and local agencies. By October, some 200 defendants had been indicted, and the case continues.

Pfizer fraud: In the largest health care fraud settlement in Department of Justice history, the pharmaceutical giant agreed in September to pay $2.3 billion to resolve charges of illegal and fraudulent promotion of its products.

Large-scale corruption: In July, 44 prominent political and religious leaders—including mayors, assemblymen, and rabbis from New Jersey and New York—were arrested in an early morning sweep and charged with political corruption and high-volume international money laundering.

Bernard Madoff: In March, the financier pled guilty to multiple counts of fraud and money laundering after bilking his clients out of billions of dollars. In June, the 71-year-old was sentenced to 150 years in prison and ordered to forfeit more than $170 billion to the government.

Mortgage fraud: In April, indictments were announced in connection with the "Dream Homes Program." The program promised to pay homeowners' mortgages in return for an up-front fee that would be invested in profitable business ventures but turned into a $70 million nightmare for more than 1,000 investors.

2009: The FBI Story Index

2009: The FBI Story Index

DIRECTOR/FBI LEADERSHIP

FIELD CASES

2009: The FBI Story Index

FOREIGN COUNTERINTELLIGENCE

GENERAL

HISTORY

2009: The FBI Story Index

INTELLIGENCE

INTERNATIONAL

LAB/OPERATIONAL TECHNOLOGY

MAJOR THEFTS/VIOLENT CRIME

2009: The FBI Story Index

ORGANIZED CRIME/DRUGS

PARTNERSHIPS

PUBLIC/COMMUNITY OUTREACH

PUBLIC CORRUPTION

2009: The FBI Story Index

RECRUITING/DIVERSITY

TECHNOLOGY

TRAINING

WHITE-COLLAR CRIME